Published by:

Faith Celebration Christian Centre
(CAPCHURCH Inc.)
1 Ekpiwhre Drive, Opposite Mosheshe Estate, Enerhen, Warri, Delta State, Nigeria.

ISBN: 978-978-51071-8-0

Printed in the Federal Republic of Nigeria

Brief Introduction

Brief Introduction

To God be the glory, in 2016, I began putting these daily devotional together to encourage and challenge my members at the Faith Celebration Christian Centre, Warri. And I also began to share these daily inspirations with friends on Facebook and WhatsApp groups; the responses were extremely encouraging. Since then, I have faithfully shared these devotionals daily; even when I am out of Nigeria. I really thank God who inspires me by the Holy Spirit to write.

I urge you to read these devotional; you have a great material in your hand that will turn your life around for good and your best will begin to manifest in next sixty days.

I thank all the members of Faith Celebration Christian Centre of the Celebration Apostolic Power Church for their availability to receive the Word of God and for their supports through the years. Thanks to my fathers in the faith; Bishop David Oyedepo, Pastor Festus Agu, Rev. Dr. Chris Oyakhilome, Dsc, DD and several others too numerous to mention for their impact in my life and ministry. I am grateful Sirs. I also appreciate my friends and family.

Special thanks to my wife and children. I love you all.

Day 1

Grow Your Faith Daily

"This book of the law shall not depart out of thy mouth; but thou shalt meditate therein day and night, that thou mayest observe to do according to all that is written therein: for then thou shalt make thy way prosperous, and then thou shalt have good success." (Joshua 1:8)

As a Christian, it is important to always remember that there is no alternative to the Word of God. Our opening scripture for today reveals God's purpose and what we need to do for a prosperous living.

Our lives must be built on the Word of God. There is no alternative. Every alternative will only lead to shaking, unstable, and eventually a collapsed life.

Matthew 7:24-27 reads: *"Therefore whosoever heareth these sayings of mine, and doeth them, I will liken him unto a wise man, which built his house upon a rock:*

And the rain descended, and the floods came, and the winds blew, and beat upon that house; and it fell not: for it was founded upon a rock.

And every one that heareth these sayings of mine, and doeth them not, shall be likened unto a foolish man, which built his house upon the sand:

And the rain descended, and the floods came, and the winds blew, and beat upon that house; and it fell: and great was the fall of it."

Apostle Paul also admonished Timothy the Bishop to hold on to the Word of God.

"Meditate upon these things; give thyself wholly to them; that thy profiting may appear to all.

Take heed unto thyself, and unto the doctrine; continue in them: for in doing this thou shalt both save thyself, and them that hear thee." (1 Timothy 4:15-16).

Since we must only live by faith as Christians, the Word of God must play a vital role in our day to day activities. We must take time to study the Word, meditate on it, and endeavor to do all that is written therein. Hallelujah!

If you want to have success in life, go for the Word of God. Know it and practice it daily. No option.

PRAYER

Dear Father in heaven, Hallowed be Thy name. Thank You for Your word that is always sufficient for me to excel in every aspect of life. Today as I meditate on Your word, I am strong and powerful, doing exploits naturally in Jesus' name.

THE BLESSING

May the glory of the Lord God Almighty decorate my life in the name of the Lord Jesus Christ.

THE INVITATION

If you haven't received Jesus as your Lord and personal Savior, pray this prayer now: *"**Dear Lord Jesus, I believe You are the Son of God and that You died for my sins. Come into my heart and make me a child of God in Jesus' name, I pray. Amen.**"*

Please read Romans 10:9-10:

"That if thou shalt confess with thy mouth the Lord Jesus, and shalt believe in thine heart that God hath raised him from the dead, thou shalt be saved.

For with the heart man believeth unto righteousness; and with the mouth confession is made unto salvation."

Day 2

Stay Safe

"So then faith cometh by hearing, and hearing by the word of God." **(Romans 10:17)**

Our opening Scripture for today says: *"...Faith cometh by hearing and hearing by the word of God."* As God's children, we must feed our faith fat with the Word of God and make it grow daily.

To grow our faith we must hear the Word of God again and again because faith comes by hearing and hearing again and again. Never become too busy that you don't have time to feed on the Word of God daily.

It is the level of your feeding on the word of God (by studying and meditating) that determines the level and strength of your faith.

We need faith to withstand the wiles of the devil. The Bible in **Ephesians 6:11** says: *"Put on the whole armour of God that ye may be able to stand against the wiles of the devil."* Among the whole armor of God that we must put on is the *"shield of faith"* according to **Ephesians 6:16:** *"Above all, taking the shield of faith, wherewith ye shall be able to quench all the fiery darts of the wicked."* It takes the Word of God in our heart to quench all the fiery darts or arrows of the wicked shot at us.

Jesus taught us about faith that is strong enough to withstand different situations and circumstances of life in **Matthew 7:24-25;** He said: *"Therefore whosoever heareth these* *sayings of mine, and doeth them, I will liken him unto a wise man, which built his house upon a rock:*

And the rain descended, and the floods came, and the winds blew, and beat upon that house; and it fell not: for it was founded upon a rock."

Remember the Bible says, ***"The just shall live by faith"*** (Romans 1:17). How then can one live by what he doesn't have? You must first build your faith to live by it.

Don't wait until there is a problem before you start building your faith. It is dangerous to do so, because (you may not be able to stand) except by divine intervention, your faith may fail or you may injure your destiny badly and life becomes difficult for you and others that are connected to you. Therefore, feed your faith daily as a Christian.

1 Peter 2:1-2 says: ***"Wherefore laying aside all malice, and all guile, and hypocrisies, and envies, and all evil speaking,***

As newborn babes, desire the sincere milk of the word, that ye may grow thereby."

Build your faith by reading, hearing, and meditating on the Word of God daily. You can have more faith.

PRAYER

Dear Father, thank You for Your word. As I feed on the Word, my faith is growing stronger and stronger and I am enjoying the overcomer's life daily in every aspect of life in Jesus' name. Amen

THE BLESSING

May I be favored and honored by God and man this day in Jesus' name.

THE INVITATION

If you haven't received Jesus as your Lord and personal Savior, pray this prayer now: *"Dear Lord Jesus, I believe You are the Son of God and that You died for my sins. Come into my heart and make me a child of God in Jesus name I pray. Amen."*

Please read Romans 10:9-10.

"That if thou shalt confess with thy mouth the Lord Jesus, and shalt believe in thine heart that God hath raised him from the dead, thou shalt be saved.

For with the heart man believeth unto righteousness; and with the mouth confession is made unto salvation."

Day 3

The Importance of Faith

"And he that doubteth is damned if he eat, because he eateth not of faith: for whatsoever is not of faith is sin." (Romans 14:23)

The Scripture above tells us about the IMPORTANCE OF FAITH. *"... For whatsoever is not of faith is sin."* Romans 14:23.

Faith must be involved in whatever we do. It is the foundation of all we do in life that pleases God. **Hebrews 11:6** reads: *"But without faith it is impossible to please him: for he that cometh to God must believe that he is, and that he is a rewarder of them that diligently seek him."*

Our man of God, the esteemed Rev. Dr. Chris Oyakhilome Dsc. DD. defined faith as: *"The response of man's spirit to the Word of God."* The book of **Romans 10:17** says: *"So then faith cometh by hearing, and hearing by the word of God."*

Going by our main scriptural text for today, anything we do without faith is not acceptable to God.

Many pray and receive no answer because FAITH is not involved.

Begin to build your faith now, don't just copy people. Copying won't work and it will not be pleasing God. For instance, when **Jeremiah 33:3** came alive in my spirit and produced faith in me, I started receiving answers to my prayers. God began to do great and mighty things that I knew not in my life and ministry. I developed a *"**fear not, God has done it**"* mentality.

I plead with you to begin to build your faith. Hear the Word of God until faith is born in your heart. Ensure you take the studying of the word as a serious business. Do all it takes now and begin to LIVE BY FAITH and you will see that it works in your life. Hallelujah!

PRAYER

Dear Father, thank You for Your love. Today, faith is growing in me as I read, study, and hear Your word in Jesus' name. I live triumphantly in every aspect of my life in Jesus' name.

THE BLESSINGS

I put upon you today, the glory of God in Jesus name. Enjoy the manifestation of God's glory in every aspect of your life in Jesus' name.

THE INVITATION

If you haven't received Jesus as your Lord and personal Savior, pray this prayer now: **Dear Lord Jesus, I believe You are the Son of God and that You died for my sins. Come into my heart and make me a child of God in Jesus' name. Amen.**

Please read Romans 10:9-10.

"That if thou shalt confess with thy mouth the Lord Jesus, and shalt believe in thine heart that God hath raised him from the dead, thou shalt be saved.

For with the heart man believeth unto righteousness; and with the mouth confession is made unto salvation."

Day 4

The Word Is Spirit and Life

"It is the spirit that quickeneth; the flesh profiteth nothing: the words that I speak unto you, they are spirit, and they are life." (John 6:63)

In today's opening scriptural text, Jesus said, ***"The word that I speak unto you, they are spirit and they are life"*** John 6:63

To have the life and the Spirit of Christ in us, we must have the Word of God in our spirit. It is the word that is Spirit quickened. It is the word that gives life or makes alive. Everyone that needs life must give quality attention to the word of God.

The more of the Word of God in you, the more you will be filled with the Spirit that quickens and gives life and divine vitamins to vitalize your body.

Begin to seriously and consistently feed yourself fat with the word of God and enjoy life in abundance. Jesus told us He came so that we might have life abundantly.

John 10:10 says: ***"The thief cometh not, but for to steal, and to kill, and to destroy: I am come that they might have life, and that they might have it more abundantly."***

Peter also said that only Jesus has the words of eternal life.

John 6:68-69: ***"Then Simon Peter answered him, Lord, to whom shall we go? Thou hast the words of eternal life.***

And we believe and are sure that thou art that Christ, the Son of the living God."

Begin to seriously study the Bible and consciously take the word in until it is all you are thinking and doing so that you will experience life, good health, wellness, and prosperity in every aspect of life.

PRAYER

Father, thank You for Your love and power that is causing me to live victoriously in this present world. I am filled with Your Spirit and life as I hear and study Your word, and as I meditate on it today in Jesus' name. My strength is increasing and my capacity has enlarged in Jesus' name.

THE BLESSING

May the hand of the Lord search out your enemies and judge them accordingly in Jesus' name. You are free indeed!

THE INVITATION

If you haven't received Jesus as your Lord and personal Savior, pray this prayer now: **Dear Lord Jesus, I believe You are the Son of God and that You died for my sins. Come into my heart and make me a child of God in Jesus' name I pray. Amen.**

Please read Romans 10:9-10.

"That if thou shalt confess with thy mouth the Lord Jesus, and shalt believe in thine heart that God hath raised him from the dead, thou shalt be saved.

For with the heart man believeth unto righteousness; and with the mouth confession is made unto salvation."

Day 5

Change Evil Pronouncements

"And Jabez was more honourable than his brethren: and his mother called his name Jabez,

Saying, Because I bare him with sorrow.

And Jabez called on the God of Israel, saying, Oh that thou wouldest bless me indeed, and enlarge my coast, and that thine hand might be with me, and that thou wouldest keep me from evil, that it may not grieve me! And God granted him that which he requested." (1 Chronicles 4:9-10)

Our opening scripture for today tells us what to do when somebody had made evil pronouncements on us in any way, we must change it using what the Word of God says in the name of the Lord Jesus Christ.

Jabez's mother gave him a name (son of sorrow). That was not good and by so made an evil pronouncement on his destiny but when he came of age and faith, he changed it by calling upon the name of the Lord God of Israel with his mouth.

Goliath also made a pronouncement against David and David changed it in the name of the Lord God of Israel according to the Bible in **1 Samuel 17:43-47: "*And the Philistine said unto David, Am I a dog, that thou comest to me with staves? And the Philistine cursed David by his gods.***

And the Philistine said to David, come to me, and I will give thy flesh unto the fowls of the air, and to the beasts of the field.

Then said David to the Philistine, Thou comest to me with a sword, and with a spear, and with a shield: but I come to thee in the name of the LORD of hosts, the God of the armies of Israel, whom thou hast defied.

This day will the LORD deliver thee into mine hand; and I will smite thee, and take thine head from thee; and I will give the carcasses of the host of the Philistines this day unto the fowls of the air, and to the wild beasts of the earth; that all the earth may know that there is a God in Israel.

And all this assembly shall know that the LORD saveth not with sword and spear: for the battle is the LORD's, and he will give you into our hands."

Don't just accept any evil pronouncements against you; use your month in agreement with your heart and make a counter declaration that you desire based on the word of God in Jesus name. Glory to God!

No matter what you see or hear, declare what the word says about you and your situation in Jesus' name.

Always use your God-given authority to cancel and change every evil pronouncement against your life, business, family, or every other thing that concerns you and it will be as you declare or pronounce in the name of the Lord and not according to what the enemy had said or pronounced.

PRAYER

Father thank you for all the rights and privileges we have in Christ. By the authority in your word, I change any and every evil pronouncement against my life and destiny in Jesus' name. I declare the evil pronouncements shall not stand in Jesus' name.

THE BLESSING

I declare and proclaim your liberty right now in Jesus' name. You are free.

THE INVITATION

If you haven't received Jesus as your Lord and personal Savior, pray this prayer now: **Dear Lord Jesus, I believe You are the Son of God and that You died for my sins. Come into my heart and make me a child of God in Jesus' name, I pray. Amen.**

Please read Romans 10:9-10.

"That if thou shalt confess with thy mouth the Lord Jesus, and shalt believe in thine heart that God hath raised him from the dead, thou shalt be saved.

For with the heart man believeth unto righteousness; and with the mouth confession is made unto salvation."

Day 6

Arise In Your Spirit And Begin To Shine

"Arise, shine; for thy light is come, and the glory of the Lord is risen upon thee." (Isaiah 60:1)

As a child of God, you are a special being, a spiritual being that God has blessed beyond measure. Why is it then that many Christians are not enjoying the enormous blessings God has bestowed upon them? The answer to this is found in our scriptural text for today. It says:

"Arise, shine; for thy light is come, and the glory of the LORD is risen upon thee." Isaiah 60:1.

Every child of God has the responsibility to rise before shining. It means to believe God and stand or rise in your spirit man and begin to do something, (the work of the word) according to James 1:25 that says *"But whoso looketh into the perfect law of liberty, and continueth therein, he being not a forgetful hearer, but a doer of the work, this man shall be blessed in his deed."*

Remember your light has already come and the glory of God has risen upon you already. The very day you received Jesus as your Savior and Lord, your destiny changed.

What are those things expected of you in His word? Begin to do them now and see how you will be shining. Glory!

Jesus said in Matthew 5:14,16:

"Ye are the light of the world. A city that is set on a hill cannot be hid.

Let your light so shine before men, that they may see your good works, and glorify your Father which is in heaven."

If only you will rise, shining will begin to manifest naturally in your life by the anointing of the Holy Spirit. Give yourself to the study of the word and consciously become a doer of the word and see yourself shining brighter and brighter.

PRAYER

Father, I thank you very much for the wonderful works you've been doing for me, today I rise and shine in your light that has risen upon me in Jesus name.

THE BLESSING

I decree today, you shall not be conquered by the power of darkness in Jesus' name.

THE INVITATION

If you haven't received Jesus as your Lord and personal Savior, pray this prayer now: **Dear Lord Jesus, I believe You are the Son of God and that You died for my sins. Come into my heart and make me a child of God in Jesus' name, I pray. Amen.**

Please read Romans 10:9-10.

"That if thou shalt confess with thy mouth the Lord Jesus, and shalt believe in thine heart that God hath raised him from the dead, thou shalt be saved.

For with the heart man believeth unto righteousness; and with the mouth confession is made unto salvation."

Day 7

Be Steadfast In The Faith

"Be sober, be vigilant; because your adversary the devil, as a roaring lion, walketh about, seeking whom he may devour:

Whom resist stedfast in the faith, knowing that the same afflictions are accomplished in your brethren that are in the world.

But the God of all grace, who hath called us unto his eternal glory by Christ Jesus, after that ye have suffered a while, make you perfect, stablish, strengthen, settle you." (1 Peter 5:8-10)

The emphasis today will be on steadfastness in the faith.

According to our opening scripture for today, Christians need to be steadfast in their faith because the devil as a roaring lion is walking about seeking for whom to devour, destroy, or kill. Our steadfast resistance in faith will give him no room to defeat or destroy us in any way. Whenever he attacks with the things (*challenges or problems*) that are common in the world, we should not forget God's word in **1 Peter 5:10** that says,

"But the God of all grace, who hath called us unto his eternal glory by Christ Jesus, after that ye have suffered a while, make you perfect, establish, strengthen, settle you."

Faith makes God real to the individual who believes the word of God and also causes the individual to enjoy the fulfillment of the promises of God in his or her life. Let us remain steadfast in our faith in God no matter what, knowing that God is with us and will deliver us from all troubles and challenges of life in due time. Hallelujah!

Always walk in victory, never forget you are different from those of the world, you are in Christ Jesus and God's promises are *"Yea and amen in Him."* Hallelujah!

2 Corinthians 5:17, *"Therefore if any man be in Christ, he is a new creature: old things are passed away; behold, all things are become new."*

You are a new creation now in Christ. Be conscious of who you are always and be steadfast in your faith.

PRAYER

Father thank You for always being there for me in Jesus' name. Let every evil bow to You in my life today in the mighty name of Jesus Christ. I walk in the light of Your word and enjoy the power of the Holy Ghost working in my life in Jesus' name. Amen

THE BLESSING

May the oil of favor come upon you afresh in Jesus' name be favored in every aspect of life in Jesus name.

THE INVITATION

If you haven't received Jesus as your Lord and personal Savior, pray this prayer now: **Dear Lord Jesus, I believe You are the Son of God and that You died for my sins. Come into my heart and make me a child of God in Jesus' name, I pray. Amen.**

Please read Romans 10:9-10.

"That if thou shalt confess with thy mouth the Lord Jesus, and shalt believe in thine heart that God hath raised him from the dead, thou shalt be saved.

For with the heart man believeth unto righteousness; and with the mouth confession is made unto salvation."

Day 8

Be Diligent In Your Business

"Seest thou a man diligent in his business? he shall stand before kings; he shall not stand before mean men." (Proverbs 22:29)

The Scripture above revealed to us how to stand before kings. Kings here connote people that matter, men of influence, honorable men, and successful people.

To stand out from the ordinary people in life, you must:

1. HAVE A BUSINESS, A WORK, OR A JOB THAT YOU ARE DOING: We cannot fold our hands and expect God to bless us or drop manna from Heaven. We must work. **Proverbs 6:6-8** says, *"Go to the ant, thou sluggard; consider her ways, and be wise:*

Which having no guide, overseer, or ruler,

Provideth her meat in the summer, and gathereth her food in the harvest."

Please answer these questions now. What is your work? What are you doing for a living and how are you doing it?

2. BE DILIGENT IN YOUR BUSINESS: We must be willing to go the extra mile, work hard, and apply different methods or strategies.

Romans 12:11 says, *"Not slothful in business; fervent in spirit; serving the Lord."*

Look for something worthwhile to do and commit yourself totally to it.

Jesus our Master and Savior said "... *My Father works and hitherto I work...*" **John 5:17.**

Read also **1 Thessalonians 4:11,** *"And that ye study to be quiet, and to do your own business, and to work with your own hands, as we commanded you."*

Always prayerfully look for what to do to make money or to profit, how to do it (the strategy), and give yourself fully to it.

God's word can never fail, if you play your part, the Holy Spirit will help you.

Read again **Proverbs 22:29** says: *"Seest thou a man diligent in his business? he shall stand before kings; he shall not stand before mean men."* Glory to God!

PRAYER

Father, thank You for Your love. Today I receive the increase of grace to discover the opportunities around me, and to work hard in my business in Jesus name. The work of my hand is prospering by the anointing of the Holy Spirit in Jesus' name.

THE BLESSING

Be fruitful all-round in the name of the Lord Jesus Christ.

THE INVITATION

If you haven't received Jesus as your Lord and personal Savior, pray this prayer now: **Dear Lord Jesus, I believe You are the Son of God and that You died for my sins. Come into my heart and make me a child of God in Jesus' name, I pray. Amen.**

Please read Romans 10:9-10.

"That if thou shalt confess with thy mouth the Lord Jesus, and shalt believe in thine heart that God hath raised him from the dead, thou shalt be saved.

For with the heart man believeth unto righteousness; and with the mouth confession is made unto salvation."

Day 9

Don't Give Up There Is Hope

"For to him that is joined to all the living there is hope: for a living dog is better than a dead lion." (Ecclesiastes 9:4)

As a Christian or even a living being, as long as you are alive on this earth, you must refuse to give up. You must keep your hope alive for success in your endeavors.

Our scriptural text for today says, ***"For to him that is joined to all the living there is hope..."***

There is hope for you reading this daily devotional right now, especially because you are alive. Say, *"Thank God, I am alive."*

Get yourself together right now and begin to happen, begin to do something worthwhile with your life, seek counsel from people who have succeeded in your area of endeavors if need be.

You can start afresh patiently; do not be discouraged or distracted by the success or failure of others. There is something beautiful ahead of you in Christ Jesus. It's a new day for you.

Jeremiah 33:3 says, ***"Call unto me, and I will answer thee, and shew thee great and mighty things, which thou knowest not."***

Call upon God right now in prayers and fasting by faith and he will answer you and show you great and mighty things that you do not know before now. Today is a new dawn for you. Glory to God!

Stick to living by the Word of God and see your life transform and change from glory to glory. No matter what you are going through right now and the circumstances that surround you, don't give up. There is hope.

PRAYER

Dear Father in heaven, hallowed be Your name. I worship You today for who You are. I thank You that by Your word I am strengthened and energized to function and to succeed again in life. Thank You for the divine ability in me in Jesus' name.

THE BLESSING

I see His glory upon you in Jesus' name. I decree and declare, no more shame for you in Jesus' name.

THE INVITATION

If you haven't received Jesus as your Lord and personal Savior, pray this prayer now: **Dear Lord Jesus, I believe You are the Son of God and that You died for my sins. Come into my heart and make me a child of God in Jesus' name, I pray. Amen.**

Please read Romans 10:9-10.

"That if thou shalt confess with thy mouth the Lord Jesus, and shalt believe in thine heart that God hath raised him from the dead, thou shalt be saved.

For with the heart man believeth unto righteousness; and with the mouth confession is made unto salvation."

Day 10

Examine Yourself If You Are In The Faith

"Examine yourselves, whether ye be in the faith; prove your own selves. Know ye not your own selves, how that Jesus Christ is in you, except ye be reprobates?" (2 Corinthians 13:5)

As Christians, we are expected to search and examine ourselves according to our opening scripture for today, because faith is personal and it's of the heart.

Examining ourselves will help us to know what we are doing wrong and to be able to make amend where necessary, to become better, and to grow without any external pressure from man.

When one fails to examine himself, he may fall into many errors or become fake or a hypocrite. We must constantly examine ourselves using the Word of God as an instrument of measurement.

Self-examination will help one to know his area of strength and weakness, as this will help in letting others help in the area of weakness and to maximize one's strength.

When we examine ourselves we are allowing the Holy Spirit to work with us and make us see our true picture and how we can change and become better in life.

Examine yourself now, make amend where necessary, and keep growing in the Lord. Always spend quality time to study and to meditate on the word of God, and you will discover the areas you need to grow in your Christian life. Please read:

2 Peter 1:5-10, "*And beside this, giving all diligence, add to your faith virtue; and to virtue knowledge;*

And to knowledge temperance; and to temperance patience; and to patience godliness;

And to godliness brotherly kindness; and to brotherly kindness charity.

For if these things be in you, and abound, they make you that ye shall neither be barren nor unfruitful in the knowledge of our Lord Jesus Christ.

But he that lacketh these things is blind, and cannot see afar off, and hath forgotten that he was purged from his old sins.

Wherefore the rather, brethren, give diligence to make your calling and election sure: for if ye do these things, ye shall never fall."

PRAYER

Father, You have allowed me to build up myself on my most holy faith, today I acknowledge my faith in You and ready to keep growing in the faith so that I can continue to do exploits for Your kingdom in Jesus' name. Amen

THE BLESSING

May the peace of the Lord preserve your heart and mind today in Jesus' name.

THE INVITATION

If you haven't received Jesus as your Lord and personal Savior, pray this prayer now: **Dear Lord Jesus, I believe You are the Son of God and that You died for my sins. Come into my heart and make me a child of God in Jesus' name, I pray. Amen.**

Please read Romans 10:9-10.

"That if thou shalt confess with thy mouth the Lord Jesus, and shalt believe in thine heart that God hath raised him from the dead, thou shalt be saved.

For with the heart man believeth unto righteousness; and with the mouth confession is made unto salvation."

Day 11

Motivate Yourself For Action

"Wherefore I put thee in remembrance that thou stir up the gift of God, which is in thee by the putting on of my hands." (2 Timothy 1:6)

The opening scripture above tells us of the instruction of the great Apostle Paul to Timothy his son in the faith. He told him to stir up the gift of God in him. Like a spoon in a cup of tea is for stirring the contents, we must have a means or an instrument of self-motivation.

As believers in Jesus Christ, we must learn how to stir up our faith, our gifts, and ourselves. This means we must be able to do something that can spur us to action. Many a time, one may be too cold, sluggish and lazy, or careless, and this may render one's gift or ability useless. There are lots we can do as children of God but it may not happen until we learn how to stir up ourselves to do the work of God.

The Bible shows us that praying in the Holy Ghost can build or stir us up within until we become motivated.

Jude 1:20 says, ***"But ye, beloved, building up yourselves on your most holy faith, praying in the Holy Ghost."***

Pray much in the tongues of the Spirit for constant self-motivation. Don't allow a dull moment.

We have to devise a means of self-motivation to pray, to fast, to render service, to win souls, and to do all that is expected of us in every aspect of life. This will make us living and winning Christians all the time.

Be conscious of who you are and your assignment in life as a Christian and begin to do what is expected of you with little or no external push or pressure in line with **Isaiah 60:1** that says, ***"Arise, shine; for thy light is come, and the glory of the LORD is risen upon thee."***

Arise, get up now, and begin to move in the right direction, the direction of the word of God. Study and meditate on the word more and be gingered within. Glory to God!

PRAYER

Father thank You for the divine ability that is in me to do exploits in life.

Today I ginger, encourage, and motivate myself by the Holy Spirit to do Your word in Jesus' name. I function in my place and enjoy peace, joy, and progress today in Jesus name

THE BLESSING

May grace announce you from this day forward in Jesus' name.

Every demonic weakness is removed out of your life now in Jesus' name.

THE INVITATION

If you haven't received Jesus as your Lord and personal Savior, pray this prayer now: **Dear Lord Jesus, I believe You are the Son of God and that You died for my sins. Come into my heart and make me a child of God in Jesus' name I pray. Amen.**

Please read Romans 10:9-10.

"That if thou shalt confess with thy mouth the Lord Jesus, and shalt believe in thine heart that God hath raised him from the dead, thou shalt be saved.

For with the heart man believeth unto righteousness; and with the mouth confession is made unto salvation."

Day 12

Make A Good Warfare By The Prophecies You Have Received

"This charge I commit unto thee, son Timothy, according to the prophecies which went before on thee, that thou by them mightest war a good warfare." (1 Timothy 1:18)

The scriptural text for today says, *"Make good warfare by the prophecies that went before on thee."* After receiving prophecies from the servant of God or the preaching of the word of God, you don't have to go and sit down but you have to war "a good warfare" by it. You have to start doing all it takes. (Look for the book, "How to receive a miracle and keep it")

You can make war by taking the following steps; affirm the word of the prophecies or declarations daily irrespective of your present situation, or by becoming committed to the things of God. **Matthew 6:33** says, ***"But seek ye first the kingdom of God, and his righteousness; and all these things shall be added unto you."*** In anticipation of the manifestation of your miracles as prophesied, do something.

At times, there may be the need for some bold steps of faith despite the perceived obstacles that may be confronting you, you just step out and start moving. Hallelujah!

For instance, after Mary the mother of Jesus received the word sent through the angel to her by God, she went to see Elizabeth because the Angel mentioned her in his message to her. **Luke 1:38-39** says, ***"And Mary said, Behold the handmaid of the Lord; be it unto me according to thy word. And the angel departed from her.***

1:39 And Mary arose in those days, and went into the hill country with haste, into a city of Juda."

Have you received a prophecy lately? Wake up and begin to pray. Affirm the word of God on your life, go into fasting, sow seeds, and take the necessary corresponding actions by the power of the Holy Spirit. That is how it works.

PRAYER

Dear Father, I worship You for who You are, the great and mighty God.

Today as I war "a good warfare" by Your word, my profit is appearing to all in Jesus name. I live by the sure word of prophecy and I am making progress daily in Jesus' name. Hallelujah!

THE BLESSING

May the glory increase daily. You shall not fail in life in the mighty name of the Lord Jesus.

THE INVITATION

If you haven't received Jesus as your Lord and personal Savior, pray this prayer now: **Dear Lord Jesus, I believe You are the Son of God and that You died for my sins. Come into my heart and make me a child of God in Jesus' name, I pray. Amen.**

Please read Romans 10:9-10.

"That if thou shalt confess with thy mouth the Lord Jesus, and shalt believe in thine heart that God hath raised him from the dead, thou shalt be saved.

For with the heart man believeth unto righteousness; and with the mouth confession is made unto salvation."

Day 13

Don't Fight Against The Truth

"For we can do nothing against the truth, but for the truth." (2 Corinthians 13:8)

As a child of God you need to know the word, embrace the truth, live by the truth, and do nothing against or contrary to the truth but for the truth according to our opening scripture for today. Don't attempt to do anything against the truth but do something for the truth. When you receive the truth and hold on to it, you will be free from so many corruptions and wrong things in this world. For instance, the Bible says in the book of **John 8:32, *"And ye shall know the truth, and the truth shall make you free."*** Only the truth can set you free from sin and its bondage. People that reject the truth will not be free nor experience freedom in their lives but will remain in bondage forever.

What is the truth? Jesus is the truth. ***"Jesus saith unto him, I am the way, the truth, and the life: no man cometh unto the Father, but by me."* John 14:6.** What the Word of God says about you is the truth. You must believe what the word says about every aspect of life and not the lies of the devil.

Remember living by the Word of God brings blessings unlimited. **James 1:25** says, ***"But whoso looketh into the perfect law of liberty, and continueth therein, he being not a forgetful hearer, but a doer of the work, this man shall be blessed in his deed."***

Don't fight nor run away from the truth as some who hate hearing the balance word of God but like lies do, and ruined themselves. **2 Timothy 3:8** says, ***"Now as Jannes and Jambres withstood Moses, so do these also resist the truth: men of corrupt minds, reprobate concerning the faith."*** Whenever the truth is preached they will get angry and fight against the truth, this is what is keeping them from doing the right things and their end is destruction. **Hosea 4:6** says, ***"My people are destroyed for lack of knowledge: because thou hast rejected knowledge, I will*** *also reject thee, that thou shalt be no priest to me: seeing thou hast forgotten the law of thy God, I will also forget thy children."*

Don't fight against the truth but accept and celebrate the truth. Always seek the truth and live by the truth. Remember truth will always remain true. Know the truth, embrace, and live by the truth. You'll be free and enjoy blessings unlimited in Christ. Hallelujah!

Hear this, ***"Get wisdom, get understanding: forget it not; neither decline from the words of my mouth. 4:6 Forsake her not, and she shall preserve thee: love her, and she shall keep thee. 4:7 Wisdom is the principal thing; therefore, get wisdom: and with all thy getting get understanding. 4:8 Exalt her, and she shall promote thee: she shall bring thee to honor, when thou dost embrace her. 4:9 She shall give to thine head an ornament of grace: a crown of glory shall she deliver to thee. 4:10 Hear, O my son, and receive my sayings; and the years of thy life shall be many."*** **Proverbs 4:5-10.**

Read your Bible and study it to **know** the truth, listen to men of God that preach the word of God in sincerity as it is without adding or removing from it for any reason, and enjoy freedom in every aspect of your life.

Accept the truth and preach the gospel of truth to others. Don't live against the truth.

PRAYERS

Father thank You for your constant love and unfailing support always.

Today as I live by the truth of Your word, my life is meaningful and it's for Your glory in Jesus' name.

THE BLESSING

Your light is shining brighter today in Jesus' name.

THE INVITATION

If you haven't received Jesus as your Lord and personal Savior, pray this prayer now: **Dear Lord Jesus, I believe You are the Son of God and that You died for my sins. Come into my heart and make me a child of God in Jesus' name, I pray. Amen.**

Please read Romans 10:9-10.

"That if thou shalt confess with thy mouth the Lord Jesus, and shalt believe in thine heart that God hath raised him from the dead, thou shalt be saved.

For with the heart man believeth unto righteousness; and with the mouth confession is made unto salvation."

Day 14

Let The Word Change Your Mind

"And be not conformed to this world: but be ye transformed by the renewing of your mind, that ye may prove what is that good, and acceptable, and perfect, will of God." (Romans 12:2)

You need to know as a child of God that until your mind is changed, your words can not change, and if your words do not change then your life can not change. If you desire your life to change, therefore, you must let the word renew or change your mind according to our opening scripture for today.

The process is like this, you give yourself to the hearing, reading, and studying of the Word and it changes your mind and your words, as you begin to speak in line with the Word of God then your life will begin to change also.

It is important that you set out to renew your mind consciously or else, your life will not be different than what it was before you received Jesus as your Savior and Lord. But when your mind is renewed by the word all you do will be in line with the word. **Colossians 3:16-17** says, *"Let the word of Christ dwell in you richly in all wisdom; teaching and admonishing one another in psalms and hymns and spiritual songs, singing with grace in your hearts to the Lord. 3:17 And whatsoever ye do in word or deed, do all in the name of the Lord Jesus, giving thanks to God and the Father by him."*

You have the responsibility to let the Word change you. You must begin to give serious attention to the Word from now on. Gather every Christian material that will help you and begin to consciously use them to experience a change of life. As you allow the Word of God, it will change your life forever. Hallelujah!

PRAYER

Dear father, thank you for your word that is loaded with the divine ability to renew our minds and to transform our lives positively. As I meditate on your word, my mind is renewed daily and I speak in line with your word today, my life is beautiful and glorious in Jesus name.

THE BLESSING

I pray God will wrap you up in his glory in Jesus' name.

THE INVITATION

If you haven't received Jesus as your Lord and personal Savior, pray this prayer now: **Dear Lord Jesus, I believe You are the Son of God and that You died for my sins. Come into my heart and make me a child of God in Jesus' name, I pray. Amen.**

Read Romans 10:9-10

Day 15

Prayer Is Essential

(In A Time Like This)

"Confess your faults one to another, and pray one for another, that ye may be healed. The effectual fervent prayer of a righteous man availeth much." (James 5:16)

"Confess to one another therefore your faults (your slips, your false steps, your offenses, your sins) and pray [also] for one another, that you may be healed and restored [to a spiritual tone of mind and heart]. The earnest (heartfelt, continued) prayer of a righteous man makes tremendous power available [dynamic in its working]." (James 5:16) (Amp)

We must give ourselves to prayers in a time like this if we are going to come out stronger as believers and as a Congregation. Prayer will make power available for us to do exploits and achieve our God-given dreams, according to our opening scripture for today. The Bible in *James 5:17-18* also revealed to us how Elijah prayed that there will be no rain and for three years and six months there was no rain. He prayed again that there should be rain and heaven gave rain. He was a man of like passion as we are, yet he prayed and got the answer. We can also pray and see the power of God working mightily for us, and in us in a time like this.

The Saints of old were men and women of prayers. They all knew God intimately. They exercised great faith and knew the power of prayer. Their successes had a lot to do with their prayer life. We can learn a lot from their prayer life and pattern. We need to know that prayer is a vital life-wire of our relationship with God. Prayer is the key that unlocks God's power in our lives and the world. Read our opening scripture for today again.

Spend quality time in prayers today, for the Church, for Celebration Apostolic Power Church Inc.; for all the members, and our brethren in other local churches of Jesus Christ all over the world. Let the power of God be made available to save, bless, heal, and deliver in all our services and evangelistic outreaches. Pray also for those in authority according to Paul's instruction in **1 Timothy 2:1-2,** *"I exhort, therefore, that, first of all, supplications, prayers, intercessions, and giving of thanks, be made for all men; 2:2 For kings, and for all that are in authority; that we may lead a quiet and peaceable life in all godliness and honesty."* We need to pray that those in authority will make the right decisions in a time like this, so that we may live and serve God in peace and remain in the will of God.

PRAY, PRAY, PRAY NOW AND ALWAYS.

Ephesians 6:18 says: *"**Praying always with all prayer and supplication in the Spirit, and watching thereunto with all perseverance and supplication for all saints**."*

PRAYER

Dear Father,thank you for your love and for the Holy Spirit that you show and gave to us. The same is working in us and through us to your praise and glory in Jesus' name. By my prayers, power is made available and I am seeing great and mighty things that I knew not in Jesus' name.

THE BLESSING

May God cause His light to shine on you today in Jesus' name. You are a wonder today in Jesus' name.

THE INVITATION

If you haven't received Jesus as your Lord and Savior, pray this prayer now: **Dear Lord Jesus, I believe you are the Son of God and that you died for me. Come into my heart and make me a child of God. I now believe you are my Savior and confess you as the Lord of my life, I am born again. Glory to God!**

Please read, Romans 10:9-10

Day 16

Opportunities And You

**"To every thing there is a season, and a time to every purpose under the heaven."
(Ecclesiastes 3:1)**

In life there are opportunities and one must understand some things about these opportunities of life, most especially as a child of God to use them for our advantage and progress in life.

Our opening scripture for today says

"To everything there is a season, and a time to every purpose under the heaven" (Ecclesiastes 3:1)

Opportunities are the special messengers and seasons that come to a man to change his life for good.

It can come in the form of a relationship, business, information, academic, and even spiritual open doors or programs. What we do with those special seasons or time of life (opportunities) determines the next level or levels of our life.

You must make good use of opportunities that come your way. Don't throw them away, don't misuse or miss them.

You can quickly ask yourself these three questions:

How will this opportunity glorify God?

How will it bless others?

How will it change my life for the better?

If the answers to these questions are positive, go ahead, and do what it takes.

Every opportunity comes with a price tag and each time we miss it and it comes around again, the price goes up.

We must therefore learn to use opportunities the first time they come because the Bible says, *"Now is the day of salvation."*

2 Corinthians 6:1-2 says "**We then, as workers together with him, beseech you also that ye receive not the grace of God in vain. 6:2 (For he saith, I have heard thee in a time accepted, and in the day of salvation have I succored thee: behold, now is the accepted me; behold, now is the day of salvation.)**"

The year 2021 is full of many opportunities, be prayerful and watchful enough to discover and to make good use of the opportunities as it comes your way and you will become better and better in Jesus name. Don't forget to depend on the Holy Spirit for divine directions concerning opportunities available when you are praying and studying the Word of God. Be quick to notice and discover opportunities and use them for your advancement in life.

PRAYER

Father, I thank you for the opportunities you've made available for me in life. I receive grace to recognize and to use correctly every opportunity that will come my way from this day in Jesus' name.

THE BLESSING

May the Lord God Almighty preserve you from all evils in Jesus' name. Enjoy greater grace this year in Jesus' name.

THE INVITATION

If you haven't received Jesus as your Lord and Savior, pray from your heart now: **Dear Lord Jesus, I believe you are the Son of God and that you died for my sins. Come into my heart and make me a child of God. I now receive you as my Savior and confess you as the Lord of my life. I am born again. Glory to God in Jesus' name. Amen.**

Read Romans 10:9-10

Day 17

Be Willing To Learn

"My people are destroyed for lack of knowledge: because thou hast rejected knowledge, I will also reject thee, that thou shalt be no priest to me: seeing thou hast forgotten the law of thy God, I will also forget thy children." (Hosea 4:6)

The Bible warned through Apostle Paul that a time will come that people will have itching ears and not willing to learn but looking for those who will say what they like to hear and not what they need to hear.

In **2 Timothy 4:3,** he said by the Holy Spirit, "*For the time will come when they will not endure sound doctrine; but after their own lusts shall they heap to themselves teachers, having itching ears.*"

God wants you as a Christian to learn, hence he made available so many facilities to facilitate the learning process in the Bible, in the Church, and the schools.

Jesus asks people to come to him and learn in **Matthew 11:28-29** he said: "*Come unto me, all ye that labor and are heavy laden, and I will give you rest. 11:29 Take my yoke upon you, and learn of me; for I am meek and lowly in heart: and ye shall find rest unto your souls.*"

Paul taught the Church a lot of things by the inspiration of the Holy Spirit, that's the reason why we have his epistles or letters in the New Testament of the Bible. (Books of Romans to Hebrews)

Don't close your heart against learning; knowledge will lead to wisdom, that is *"insight into knowledge"* according to our leader in Christ, Rev Chris Oyakhilome PhD, DD. of Christ Embassy.

Lack of knowledge leads to destruction according to our opening scripture for today. (**Hosea 4:6**) Therefore embrace knowledge now and watch how your life will turn around for the better. Hallelujah!

PRAYER

Father, I thank you for constant revelations of your word by the Holy Spirit. By your Word, I am inspired and empowered to live victorious in Christ Jesus. Amen

THE BLESSING

May all that pursue you for evil stumble and fall in Jesus' name.

THE INVITATION

If you haven't received Jesus Christ as your Lord and Savior, pray this prayer now: ***Dear Lord Jesus, I believe you are the Son of God and that you died for my sins. Come into my heart and make me a child of God in Jesus' name. I now received you as my Lord and Savior. I am born again. Glory!***

Please read Romans 10:9-10

Day 18

Do The Necessary

"His mother saith unto the servants, Whatsoever he saith unto you, do it." (John 2:5)

Many church people don't want to do anything in life and yet want to succeed and make it big, (by "prayer" alone) but the word of God didn't teach us to just fold our hands, neglect our responsibility and be useless in any way, rather he admonished and commanded us to work and do the necessary in every aspect of our lives as believers. Our opening scripture for today revealed to us what Mary the mother of Jesus said to the servants when the wine got finished at the wedding in Canaan of Galilee, *"Whatsoever he saith unto you, do it."* This shows to us we must get involve and engage ourselves with doing the necessary as expected by God.

There are things you must do as a person, in your marriage, business, ministry, and relationship etc. Don't ever leave God to do what is expected of you to do. It is an error and a lie from the bottom of hell. Get up, put on your strength, and start doing the necessary now. The Bible says in **James 2:14-17: "*What doth it profit, my brethren, though a man say he hath faith, and have not works? Can faith save him? 2:15 If a brother or sister be naked, and destitute of daily food, 2:16 And one of you say unto them, depart in peace, be ye warmed and filled; notwithstanding ye give them not those things which are needful to the body; what doth it profit? 2:17 Even so faith, if it hath not works, is dead, being alone.*"**

The danger of not doing the necessary for whatever reason is enumerated in this portion of the scripture, **Proverbs 6:6-11: "*Go to the ant, thou sluggard; consider her ways, and be wise: 6:7 Which having no guide, overseer, or ruler, 6:8 Provideth her meat in the summer, and gathereth her food in the harvest.*"**

6:9 How long wilt thou sleep, O sluggard? When wilt thou arise out of thy sleep? 6:10 Yet a little sleep, a little slumber, a little folding of the hands to sleep: 6:11 So shall thy poverty come as one that travelleth, and thy want as an armed man."

Idleness and failure to work when necessary will lead to poverty.

Just like Jesus, find out what you need to do in any aspect of your life and start doing it. But Jesus answered them, *"My Father worketh hitherto, and I work."* (John 5:17)

Work, work, work, do the necessary.

PRAYER

Dear Father, thank you for all you have done in my life and for the great opportunity to be alive and well so that I could function in my place. As I work on my work, I prospered by the anointing of the Holy Spirit for all my labor produces a great harvest in Jesus' name.

BLESSING

May the Lord God Almighty grant you speed in achieving your goals this month and year in Jesus' name.

THE INVITATION

If you haven't received Jesus Christ as your Lord and Savior, pray this prayer now: *Dear Lord Jesus, I believe you are the Son of God and that you died for my sins. Come into my heart and make me a child of God in Jesus' name. I now received you as my Savior and confess you as the Lord of my life. I am born again. Glory!*

Please read Romans 10:9-10

Day 19

Know The Word Personally

"Study to shew thyself approved unto God, a workman that needeth not to be ashamed, rightly dividing the word of truth." (Timothy 2:15)

God wants you to know the word personally as a Christian according to our opening scripture for today; *"Study to show yourself..."* (2 Timothy 2:15).

There is a need for the individual Christian to know the Word of God as it is in the Bible personally.

To know the word personally you must, study the Word and meditate on it like the Psalmist. **Psalms 1:2** says: *"But his delight is in the law of the LORD; and in his law doth he meditate day and night."*

To study is different than just reading, in studying the word; you pay close attention to the Word and try to understand fully what the Word is saying to you personally or to others.

Knowing the Word for yourself brings freedom, Jesus says in **John 8:32:** *"And ye shall know the truth, and the truth shall make you free."*

It will also make you prosper and have good success in life according to **Joshua 1:8**, that says: *"This book of the law shall not depart out of thy mouth; but thou shalt meditate therein day and night, that thou mayest observe to do according to all that is written therein: for then thou shalt make thy way prosperous, and then thou shalt have good success."*

When you know the word personally and live by the word, you will be blessed in your work and walk of faith.

James 1:25 says: *"But whoso looketh into the perfect law of liberty, and continueth therein, he being not a forgetful hearer, but a doer of the work, this man shall be blessed in his deed."*

When you know the word personally, it will make you establish and stable. **Ephesians 4:14** says: *"That we henceforth be no more children, tossed to and fro, and carried about with every wind of doctrine, by the sleight of men, and cunning craftiness, whereby they lie in wait to deceive."*

PRAYER

Dear Father, thank you very much for the opportunity to read, study and to understand your word. Today as I study your word, I am increasing in knowledge of the truth and experiencing freedom in every aspect of my life in Jesus' name.

THE BLESSING

May your eyes of understanding be enlightened this day and month in Jesus' name.

THE INVITATION

If you haven't received Jesus Christ as your Lord and Savior, pray this prayer now: ***Dear Lord Jesus, I believe you are the Son of God and that you died for my sins. Come into my heart and*** *make me a child of God in Jesus' name. I now received you as my Lord and Savior. I am born again. Glory!*

Please read Romans 10:9-10

Day 20

Live Daily In Christ Alone As A Christian

"Therefore if any man be in Christ, he is a new creature: old things are passed away; behold, all things are become new." (2 Corinthians 5:17)

As a Christian, you don't have another life but life in Christ. Christ is a place; in him is our dwelling place. The opening scripture for today says, in Christ, we are a new creature, and we have a new life. Living outside Christ as a Christian is living outside your place, it is death and frustration. For instance, a fish will not survive outside water because it was not the habitation designed for it by God.

Don't attempt to live outside Christ, it won't work. It can complicate your life and put you in trouble. You must always live by the Word of God alone. **Romans 6:1-4 says: "*What shall we say then? Shall we continue in sin, that grace may abound? 6:2 God forbid. How shall we, that are dead to sin, live any longer therein? 6:3 Know ye not, that so many of us as were baptized into Jesus Christ were baptized into his death? 6:4 Therefore we are buried with him by baptism into death: that like as Christ was raised up from the dead by the glory of the Father, even so we also should walk in newness of life.*"**

Jesus also told us in **John 15:4: "*Abide in me, and I in you. As the branch cannot bear fruit of itself, except it abides in the vine; no more can ye, except ye abide in me.*"** Until I you abide in Christ Jesus, you can never be fulfilled because outside him there is no life for a child of God. In Christ is a fulfillment as you see yourself manifesting the fruit of a recreated spirit. ***Galatians 5:22-23 says: "But the fruit of the Spirit is love, joy, peace, longsuffering, gentleness, goodness, faith, 5:23 Meekness, temperance: against such there is no law.*"**

It is up to me to surrender fully to the Lordship of Jesus and live in and for him alone like Apostle Paul who said in **Galatians 2:20: "*I am crucified with Christ: nevertheless, I live; yet not I, but Christ liveth in me: and the life which I now live in the flesh I live by the faith of the Son of God, who loved me, and gave himself for me.*"**

When you discover yourself stepping out of him (*living outside his will and words*) return quickly as you confess your sins and receive cleansing by his blood and move on in the right direction (**1 John 1:9**).

Keep living permanently in Christ's environment; doing the word of God and your life will be full of his glory and for his glory alone. **Galatians 5:1** says, "***Stand fast therefore in the liberty wherewith Christ hath made us free, and be not entangled again with the yoke of bondage***."

Live only a Christian's life; don't live like the world around you and you will enjoy your new life in Christ. "***What shall we say then? Shall we continue in sin, that grace may abound? 6:2 God forbid. How shall we, that are dead to sin, live any longer therein? 6:3 Know ye not, that so many of us as were baptized into Jesus Christ were baptized into his death? 6:4 Therefore we are buried with him by baptism into death: that like as Christ was raised up from the dead by the glory of the Father, even so we also should walk in newness of life***." (**Romans 6:1-4**)

PRAYER

Dear father, thank you for the glorious life we have in Christ Jesus. My connection with him makes my life so beautiful beyond explanation. I rejoice in him daily as I live in him and for him alone in all that I do. My life is for his glory and I make progress daily by the power of the Holy Ghost in Jesus' name. Hallelujah!

THE BLESSINGS

May the power of God secure you from all evils in Jesus' name.

THE INVITATION

If you haven't received Jesus Christ as your Lord and Savior, pray this prayer now*: **Dear Lord Jesus, I believe you are the Son of God and that you died for my sins. Come into my heart and make me a child of God in Jesus' name. I now received you as my Lord and Savior. I am born again. Glory!***

Please read Romans10:9-10

Day 21

Refuse To Be Discouraged

"Have not I commanded thee? Be strong and of a good courage; be not afraid, neither be thou dismayed: for the Lord thy God is with thee whithersoever thou goest." (Joshua 1:9)

The opening scriptural text for today tells us by the Holy Spirit to be strong and of a good courage. Notice it didn't say God will make you strong and make you courageous but it says; *"Be strong and of a good courage";* It is a command.

You are to be strong and of a good courage, you must refuse to be discouraged no matter what, after all, there is no failure or weakness in God. As a child of God therefore you must refuse to be discouraged. Always say, *"I refuse to be discouraged but I choose to be courageous in Jesus' name."*

Whenever you encounter anything or anyone that wants to discourage you in life, just remember the Word of God and refuse to be discouraged. Choose to obey God instead of the circumstances or the situations that are not satisfactory to you.

The book of **Romans 8:28** says: *"**And we know that all things work together for good to them that love God, to them who are the called according to his purpose.**"* That situation and circumstance are working together for your good because you love the Lord and you are called by him.

Listen to the word of God, *"**All things work together for good,**"* your good as a child of God. You may not see or understand how, yet God's word is true.

One thing that will help you to be strong and courageous is the Word of God, keep the word in your heart, and keep confessing it with your mouth always. The more of the Word you have, the more you are bold and courageous. Hallelujah!

Get up from the inside of you and begin to do the necessary. Go after your assignments in the strength of the Lord Jesus Christ. Never be discouraged again. Glory to God!

PRAYER

Dear Father, thank you for your words of power. Today I receive your word into my heart and confess with my mouth that I am bold and courageous in the name of the Lord Jesus Christ. I refuse to be discouraged for any reason because you are always with me in Jesus' name. Amen

THE BLESSING

I pray you will triumph over every attack of the wicked and unreasonable men in the name of the Lord Jesus Christ.

THE INVITATION

If you haven't received Jesus as your Lord and Savior, pray this prayer now:

Dear Lord Jesus, I believe you are the Son of God and that you died for my sins. Come into my heart and make me a child of God in Jesus' name. I confess Jesus as my Savior and Lord, I am born again and now a child of God in Jesus name.

Read Romans 10:9-10.

Day 22

Let The Word Of Christ Dwell In You Richly

"Let the word of Christ dwell in you richly in all wisdom; teaching and admonishing one another in psalms and hymns and spiritual songs, singing with grace in your hearts to the Lord." (Colossians 3:16)

The Scripture above tells us what should dwell or occupy our mind and spirit; it is THE WORD OF CHRIST.

As a Christian, we must endeavor to know the word; we must consciously load ourselves with the word of Christ daily.

Words are very powerful, the words that occupy our minds is what will determine our actions and our behaviors. If we desire to walk in newness of life, then we must load ourselves with the Word of God.

Make reading, hearing, and meditating the word of God your incurable habit. The book of **Joshua 1:8** says: "***This book of the law shall not depart out of thy mouth; but thou shalt meditate therein day and night, that thou mayest observe to do according to all that is written therein: for then thou shalt make thy way prosperous, and then thou shalt have good success.***"

Remember again that **Colossians 3:16** tells us that the word will make us have all wisdom, and also help us to teach and admonish one another. It is a beautiful thing when believers come together sharing the Scriptures. The world talks about what filled their hearts. We must think and talk about the Word of God. It must not depart out of our mouth and our mind. Our actions must be based on the Word of God.

The Holy Spirit is always there to remind us what we have learned; we can depend on Him to help us remember the word of God.

Get serious with the word of Christ now that you are in Him.

1 Peter 2:2-3 says: "*As newborn babes, desire the sincere milk of the word, that ye may grow thereby. 2:3 If so be ye have tasted that the Lord is gracious.*" The word in you will determine how strong you are in Christ and how much your life is conforming to the Word of God.

PRAYER

Father, I thank you today for the light of your word that is lighting my path. I received grace to load my heart with your word in Jesus' name. Father, your word; the Bible is very attractive to me afresh as I study, hear and meditate on it in Jesus name.

THE BLESSINGS

May the doors of unusual favor open up for you today in Jesus' name.

INVITATION TO JESUS

If you haven't received Jesus as your Savior, pray this prayer now: **Lord Jesus, I believe that you are the Son of God and that you died for my sins. Come into my heart and make me a child of God. I now believe you as my Savior and as confess you as the Lord of my life. I am born again. Hallelujah! In Jesus' name. Amen.**

Please read Romans 10:9-10

Day 23

Pay Attention To Little Things

(The Process)

"Take us the foxes, the little foxes, that spoil the vines: for our vines have tender grapes."
(Song of Solomon 2:15)

At subsequent times, we focus on big things of life only without paying attention to the process of achieving them and as a result create problems that make life unbearable, difficult or complicated because we neglect to pay attention to little details that are necessary on a daily or weekly basis.

Our scriptural text for today showed us the danger of neglecting little foxes that spoils the vines.

Little things are much important than big things because they cumulate to form big things. For instance, we say one hundred thousand dollars, not just a thousand dollars because it will be confusing, one in many places formed the thousands so we count how many thousands we are talking about to make it sound meaningful.

The little things in life are powerful, pay absolute attention to them; they form bigger things of life. *Matthew 17:20: "And Jesus said unto them, Because of your unbelief: for verily I say unto you, if ye have faith as a grain of mustard seed, ye shall say unto this mountain, Remove hence to yonder place; and it shall remove; and nothing shall be impossible unto you."* Faith as a grain of mustard seed to move a mountain!

I exhort you this morning to begin to focus on the little things in your life, home, business, and in every other aspect this year. If you neglect little things, achieving bigger things may become difficult. So, organize your resources, home, money, your day to day life etc., and see yourself achieving your goals this year and beyond.

PRAYER

Dear Father in heaven. How great thou art, I worship you today, and thank you for your word. As I pay attention to little things I achieve bigger and greater things by the anointing of the Holy Spirit in Jesus' name.

THE BLESSING

The Lord fills you with wisdom and grace to eat honey out of this year in Jesus' name.

THE INVITATION

If you haven't received Jesus Christ as your Lord and Savior, pray this prayer now: ***Dear Lord Jesus, I believe you are the Son of God and that you died for my sins. Come into my heart and make me a child of God in Jesus' name. I now received you as my Lord and Savior. I am born again. Glory!***

Please read Romans 10:9-10

Day 24

Don't Give Up There Is Hope

"For to him that is joined to all the living there is hope: for a living dog is better than a dead lion." (Ecclesiastes 9:4)

As a Christian or even a living being, as long as you are alive on this earth, you must refuse to give up; you must keep your hope alive for success in your endeavors.

Our scriptural text for today says; "***For to him that is joined to all the living there is hope.***"

There is hope for you that is reading this daily devotional right now, most especially because you are alive; say, *"Thank God, I am alive."*

Get yourself together right now and begin to happen, begin to do something worthwhile with your life, seek counsel from people who have succeeded in your area of endeavors if need be.

Start afresh patiently, never be discouraged or distracted by the success or failure of others. There is something beautiful ahead of you in Christ Jesus. It's a new day for you.

Jeremiah 33:3 says: "***Call unto me, and I will answer thee, and shew thee great and mighty things, which thou knowest not.***"

Call upon God right now in prayers and fasting by faith and he will answer you and show you great and mighty things that you know not before now. Today is a new dawn for you. Glory to God!

Stick to living by the Word of God and see your life transform and change from glory to glory. No matter what you are going through right now and the circumstances that surround you, don't give up, there is hope. Hallelujah!

PRAYER

Dear Father in heaven, hallow be your name. I worship you today for who you are. I thank you that by your word I am strengthened and energized to function and to succeed again in life. Thank you for the divine ability in me in Jesus' name.

THE BLESSING

I see his glory upon you in Jesus' name. I decree and declare no more shame for you in Jesus' name.

THE INVITATION

If you haven't received Jesus Christ as your Lord and Savior, pray this prayer now: ***Dear Lord Jesus, I believe you are the Son of God and that you died for my sins. Come into my heart and make me a child of God in Jesus' name. I now received you and I now confess you as the Lord and Savior of my life. I am born again. Glory!***

Please read Romans 10:9-10.

Day 25

Grow Your Faith It Will Work For You

"So then faith cometh by hearing, and hearing by the word of God." (Romans 10:17)

As God's children by faith in the Lord Jesus Christ, we have a measure of faith given to us by God in our hearts according to **Romans 12:3: *"For I say, through the grace given unto me, to every man that is among you, not to think of himself more highly than he ought to think; but to think soberly, according as God hath dealt to every man the measure of faith."***

The opening scripture for today says that faith cometh by hearing the word of God. Our faith must be fed to keep it strong, healthy, and active. Faith without works (corresponding actions) is dead according to **James 2:26: "*For as the body without the spirit is dead, so faith without works is dead also*."**

To grow and keep our faith alive, strong and active, it is absolutely necessary to keep feeding it with the Word of God. We must read and read the word of God continuously. Hear the Word of God again and again. The book of **Romans 10:17** says: "*So then faith cometh by hearing, and hearing by the word of God*."

As we go on in the year and this trying period in the world, gather all the necessary materials needed, materials such as devotionals, Christian books, audio and video messages (CDs, DVDs), etc., and start using them.

Go to Church to listen to the preaching and teaching of the Word of God by your man of God. Write down the messages in your jotter or notebook. Return home to read through again and meditate on the word so that you can become a doer of it. (Joshua 1:8). Have devotional materials you can use daily and quality time set aside to seriously study, meditate on the word, and to pray.

There is much you can do or achieve with your faith in life if you feed and build it strong. Jesus revealed what you should do with your faith and what your faith would do for you in **Mark 16:17-18**: "***And these signs shall follow them that believe; In my name shall they cast out devils; they shall speak with new tongues; 16:18 They shall take up serpents; and if they drink any deadly thing, it shall not hurt them; they shall lay hands on the sick, and they shall recover***." Don't see and settle for less for your life.

It is time to begin to feed the measure (seed) of faith that made you believed and received Jesus as Savior and Lord of your life in the first place with more of the ever sure word of God.

The quality of your faith will determine the quality of the life you live.

PRAYER

Dear Father, I thank you once more for your word. As I feed my faith by reading and meditating in your word, my faith is growing stronger and stronger, increasing and increasing in Jesus' name. I do exploits this day for this is my day in Jesus' name. Hallelujah.

THE BLESSING

May your faith grow stronger and stronger to enjoy daily victory in Jesus' name.

THE INVITATION

If you haven't received Jesus as your Lord and Savior, say this prayer now: ***Lord Jesus, I believe you are the Son of God and that you died for my sins. Come into my heart and make me a child of God. I now receive you as my Savior and confess you as the Lord of my life. I am born again. Glory! Amen.***

Please read Romans10:9-10

Day 26

When Praying In Tongues Is In Place

"Confess your faults one to another, and pray one for another, that ye may be healed. The effectual fervent prayer of a righteous man availeth much." (James 5:16)

According to the second part of the scriptural text above, "*The effectual, fervent prayer of a righteous man avails much*." It means your effectual and fervent prayer works as a Christian. Therefore, we need to pray especially in tongues of the Holy Spirit if we are going to see the great changes will desire.

WHAT THE BIBLE SAYS ABOUT PRAYING IN TONGUES

Romans 8:26:

"*Likewise the Spirit also helpeth our infirmities: for we know not what we should pray for as we ought: but the Spirit itself maketh intercession for us with groanings which cannot be uttered.*"

1 Corinthians 14:1:

"For if I pray in an unknown tongue, my spirit prayeth, but my understanding is unfruitful."

 1 Corinthians 14:4

"He that speaketh in an unknown tongue edifieth himself; but he that prophesieth edifieth the church."

Jude 1:20

"But ye, beloved, building up yourselves on your most holy faith, praying in the Holy Ghost."

When praying in tongues is in place there will be rampant miracles, testimonies, fruitfulness, growth, increase, cheap victory over enemies, and building up in the faith.

TO PRAY IN TONGUES

Receive and be filled with the Holy Spirit Desire to pray in tongues.

Listen to the inner man.

Practice praying in tongues and grow in it as you pray in tongues openly.

Remember it is you who will speak in tongues as the Holy Spirit prompts you from within. Hallelujah!

Make good use of this provision in a time like this and make mysterious living, progress, and grace available for yourself and others. Glory to God!

PRAYER

Dear Father, I thank you because of who you are and for the wonderful provision of prayers. As I pray I make power available for the change that I desire in the name of the Lord Jesus Christ.

THE BLESSING

I pray for you today, your appointment with failure is terminated in Jesus' name.

THE INVITATION

If you haven't received Jesus as your Lord and personal Savior, pray this prayer now: *Dear Lord Jesus, I believe you are the Son of God and that you died for my sins. Come into my heart and make me a child of God in Jesus' name, I pray. Amen.*

Please read. Romans 10:9-10

Day 27

Abide In Christ Always

"Abide in me, and I in you. As the branch cannot bear fruit of itself, except it abide in the vine; no more can ye, except ye abide in me." (John 15:4)

The opening scripture for today tells us the word of our Lord and Savior Jesus Christ, *"ABIDE IN ME."* As Christians, we need to abide in Jesus continually if we are going to bear fruits and overcome continually in this world.

We must never stray away from Him; we must listen to Him and do His words always.

Jesus stated it clearly; we can do nothing without Him. Read the opening scripture for today again.

Many people have no time for the Word of God or time for praying continually but they pray once in a while and therefore give the devil chance to tamper with their destiny.

We must abide in Him always by being prayerful and watchful.

Ephesians 6:18: *"Praying always with all prayer and supplication in the Spirit, and watching thereunto with all perseverance and supplication for all saints."*

Romans 10:17: *"So then faith cometh by hearing, and hearing by the word of God."* Fellowship in church regularly through every available means or platform.

Hebrews 10:25 says *"Not forsaking the assembling of ourselves together, as the manner of some is; but exhorting one another: and so much the more, as ye see the day approaching."*

Value the ministry of your pastor according to the Bible; **Hebrews 13:7:** *"Remember them which have the rule over you, who have spoken unto you the word of God: whose faith follow, considering the end of their conversation."*

We must consciously apply the Word of God to our actions. **Joshua 1:8:** *"This book of the law shall not depart out of thy mouth; but thou shalt meditate therein day and night, that thou mayest observe to do according to all that is written therein: for then thou shalt make thy way prosperous, and then thou shalt have good success*." When we miss it or fall in sin, we must acknowledge our sins, confess and repent of them for forgiveness and restoration of fellowship. The Bible says: *"But if we confess our sins to God, he will keep his promise and do what is right: he will forgive us our sins and purify us from all our wrongdoing."* **1 John 1:9**(GNB)

If you want to enjoy His bests in life, you must ABIDE IN JESUS CHRIST always by constant meditation in the word and conscious application of it to all you do. Hallelujah!

PRAYER

Father, in the name of Jesus Christ I thank you, for your constant love and support that sustain and keep me living victoriously in life. Today I consciously abide in your Son Jesus through the word and my life is from glory to glory in Jesus' name. Amen

THE BLESSING

May you enjoy the victory of Christ in every aspect of your life in Jesus' name.

THE INVITATION

If you are not yet saved, say this prayer now: ***Dear Lord Jesus Christ, I believe you are the Son of God and that you died for my sins. Come into my heart and make me a child of God. I now receive you as my Savior and confess you as the Lord of my life. I am born again. Glory!***

Please read Romans 10:9-10

Day 28

Use Your Tongue To Create Good Days For Yourself

"For he that will love life, and see good days, let him refrain his tongue from evil, and his lips that they speak no guile." 1 Peter 3:10

The opening scripture for today shows us how to see or have good days. It says, if you love to live and want to see good days, USE YOUR TONGUE WISELY. Speak what you want or desire to see. Don't use the wrong words. For example, don't say, "I am sick", "I am broke", "I am dying", and such negative words, rather say, "I am rich", "I am blessed", "I am strong", "I am prosperous" and "I am healthy"; and such good and positive words.

As I always like to say, *"Every man is his own best prophet."* Learn to use your tongue/mouth to prophesy your desired future. Begin to speak in line with the Word of God for your life consistently. Stop lying, don't live a pretentious life, live a very straight forward life, whenever you fall into sin, confess your sin, and sincerely repent of them. Keep your future secure by consciously doing what it takes.

No matter what you see or are going through, begin to speak what you need to see or where you want to be and the anointing of the Holy Spirit will bring it to pass according to the Word of God. From today begin to speak to create your beautiful tomorrow, things can change for good. **Psalms 34:12-13** says, *"What man is he that desireth life, and loveth many days, that he may see good? 34:13 Keep thy tongue from evil, and thy lips from speaking guile."*

Begin to speak positively and back your confession with positive actions and your future will be beautiful. Do it. It works!

PRAYER

Dear Father, I thank you for forgiving me every wrong confession and any evil word spoken into my future in Jesus' name. Thank you for the blood of Jesus that is erasing those evil words right now in Jesus' name. I have a beautiful future in Jesus' name.

THE BLESSINGS

May your days be beautified with the beauty of the Lord God Almighty in Jesus' name. I put His name upon you today in Jesus' name. You are blessed.

THE INVITATION

If you haven't received Jesus as your Lord and Savior, say this prayer now: ***Lord Jesus, I believe you are the son of God and that you died for my sins. Come into my heart and make me a child of God. I believe you as my Savior and confess you as the Lord of my life. I am born again. Glory!***

Please read Romans 10:9-10

Day 29

Put The Things Of God First In Your Life

"But seek ye first the kingdom of God, and his righteousness; and all these things shall be added unto you." (Matthew 6:33)

The scripture above says, *"Seek ye first the kingdom of God."* As children of God, we must live by the Word of God if we are going to see the manifestations of His blessing in our lives. To have all that we need supply or added to us, we must get our priority right.

The first thing to do is to seek God's kingdom and the principles of the kingdom. Once this is in place every other thing would come supernaturally.

Jesus said we should not be worried about some things at all because God knows we need them and He is willing to supply them.

Matthew 6:31-32: "*Therefore take no thought, saying, what shall we eat? or, what shall we drink? or, Wherewithal shall we be clothed? 6:32 (For after all these things do the Gentiles seek:) for your heavenly Father knoweth that ye have need of all these things.*" Glory to God!

From now on, don't put yourself or your needs first anymore, but put God first in every aspect of life no matter what, and see how your life will begin to be prosperous and go from glory to glory. Hallelujah!

PRAYER

Father, thank you for helping me by the Holy Spirit to put your interest first in my life, and as I so I enjoy the blessings of the Lord in every aspect of my life in Jesus name.

THE BLESSING

May He that lifted the head of His people Israel, lift your head and help you stand in Jesus' name.

THE INVITATION

If you haven't received Jesus as your Lord and Savior, pray this prayer now: ***Dear Lord Jesus, I believe you are the Son of God, and that you died for my sins. Come into my heart and make me a child of God as I received you now.***

Please read Romans 10:9-10

Day 30

Remain Committed To The Word Of God

"Then said Jesus to those Jews which believed on him, If ye continue in my word, then are ye my disciples indeed." (John 8:31)

"Therefore we ought to give the more earnest heed to the things which we have heard, lest at any time we should let them slip." (Hebrews 2:1)

As a Christian, you can only live and function correctly by faith and faith comes by hearing the Word because Christian faith is based on the Word of God only.

To benefit from the Word and to live correctly and win continually, you need to give yourself totally to the Word according to our opening scriptures for today. You must study it daily.

2 Timothy 2:15 also says, "*Study to shew thyself approved unto God, a workman that needeth not to be ashamed, rightly dividing the word of truth.*"

You must meditate on the Word continually according to **Joshua 1:8** that says, "*This book of the law shall not depart out of thy mouth; but thou shalt meditate therein day and night, that thou mayest observe to do according to all that is written therein: for then thou shalt make thy way prosperous, and then thou shalt have good success.*"

You can only boast about knowing the Word when the Word so richly dwells in you and it is only the allowed thought in your mind. **Colossians 3:16** says, "*Let the word of Christ dwell in you richly in all wisdom; teaching and admonishing one another in psalms and hymns and spiritual songs, singing with grace in your hearts to the Lord.*"

Remember you are not born again to be like the unbelievers who live only to please their flesh; (only to make money and acquire material or worldly things), but to glorify God in every aspect of your life, living by faith alone in this world as a citizen of Heaven and an Ambassador of Christ, in another word Jesus becomes the Boss of your life.

Philippians 2:10-11 says, "*That at the name of Jesus every knee should bow, of things in heaven, and things in earth, and things under the earth; 2:11 And that every tongue should confess that Jesus Christ is Lord, to the glory of God the Father.*"

PRAYER

Father, thank you for your great love for all men and especially for those who believe. By your word, I move from glory to glory according to the operation of the Holy Spirit in my life. I'm so blessed and favored in Christ Jesus in Jesus' name.

THE BLESSING

May the word of God increase mightily and prevail in your life in Jesus' name.

THE INVITATION

If you haven't received Jesus Christ as your Lord and Savior, pray this prayer now: ***Dear Lord Jesus, I believe you are the Son of God and that you died for my sins. Come into my heart and make me a child of God in Jesus' name. I now received you as Savior and confess you as my Lord of my life. I am born again. Glory!***

Please read Romans10:9-10

Day 31

Respond To The Word Of God For Your Miracle

"And it came to pass, that, as the people pressed upon him to hear the word of God, he stood by the lake of Gennesaret,

And saw two ships standing by the lake: but the fishermen were gone out of them, and were washing their nets.

And he entered into one of the ships, which was Simon's, and prayed him that he would thrust out a little from the land. And he sat down, and taught the people out of the ship.

Now when he had left speaking, he said unto Simon, Launch out into the deep, and let down your nets for a draught.

And Simon answering said unto him, Master, we have toiled all the night, and have taken nothing: nevertheless at thy word I will let down the net.

And when they had this done, they inclosed a great multitude of fishes: and their net brake."
(Luke 5:1-6)

The scripture above narrated to us a brief story of Peter's encounter with Jesus; the miracle worker, when he was to preach to people at the lake of Gennesaret. It tells us how Jesus borrowed the fishing boat of Peter to use, in other to give a little space between himself and the people so they could hear him. After he finished preaching he told Peter to launch his fishing net into the deeps to be able to catch fishes; even though it was not naturally an appropriate time because it was during the day time. Peter put up a little professional argument that they've toiled all night and caught nothing, but later he changed his mind and lower the net into the sea according to the word of Jesus Christ. When he lowered the net by faith in the word in response to Jesus' instructions, he supernaturally caught many fishes even though it was during the day time.

Like Peter, we must learn how to *RESPOND TO THE WORD OF GOD* so that we'll experience the blessings of the power in the word of God in our lives personally.

When we hear or read the word we must consciously respond to the Word of God by acting on it. This will guarantee constant miracles in our lives. Glory to God.

PRAYER

Dear Father, I thank you for the glorious life you've given us. By the anointing of the Holy Spirit, I am energized to respond positively to your word from this day forward in Jesus' name. As I listened to your word and response, I am experiencing the supernatural increase, provision, and protection in Jesus' name. All my needs are met in Jesus' name. Hallelujah!

THE BLESSING

As you step out today, may you enjoy every good thing in this day in Jesus' name.

THE INVITATION

If you haven't received Jesus as your Lord and Savior, pray this prayer from your heart now: *Dear Lord Jesus, I believe you are the Son of God and that you died for my sins and rose again for my justification. Come into my heart and make me a child of God. I now believe and confess you as the Savior of my soul and the Lord of my life. I'm born again and now a child of God. Glory!*

Please read Romans 10: 9-10

Day 32

Your Personal Development Is Your Responsibility

"Study to shew thyself approved unto God, a workman that needeth not to be ashamed, rightly dividing the word of truth." (2 Timothy 2:15)

The opening scripture for today simply gave a command, *"Study to show yourself approved unto God"*

Which means, we must endeavor to study and develop ourselves or else we will not become all we could become, but we would be living below standard and maybe copying everyone and everything that we see in others without a proper understanding of the reason for doing it.

When we develop ourselves, we will not be carried about with every wind of doctrines of men. **Ephesians 4:14: *That we henceforth be no more children, tossed to and fro, and carried about with every wind of doctrine, by the sleight of men, and cunning craziness, whereby they lie in wait to deceive."*** We will be well established in the faith and our affairs of life. Stop trying to be like everyone else.

Grow from the inside out and become the best and improved you in your Christian life, marriage, business, management of your resources, etc.

Apostle Paul said in **1 Corinthians 13:11: *"When I was a child, I spake as a child, I understood as a child, I thought as a child: but when I became a man, I put away childish things."*** Now it is your turn to grow up and put away childish things.

FOR PERSONAL DEVELOPMENT TO TAKE PLACE:

Desire to grow and develop or to grow into maturity daily. Read and study the Bible.

Read profitable books.

Listen to the wise and Godly counsels of your pastor and counsels through books and messages on DVDs etc.

Avoid evil association with those that live ungodly life and never attempt to develop themselves.

Be willing to grow.

Remember you can become better than what you are now.

As you continue to do what brings personal development, you'll see yourself improving spiritually and naturally to the glory of God.

Use this time to read, discover, and develop yourself. Let the better you within show forth. Learn something new that could make you better than before. Don't waste this precious opportunity to develop yourself. Glory to God!

PRAYER

Dear Father, I thank you for the opportunity to grow and become mature as a Christian. I set my heart to study your word this season in Jesus name. I am coming out stronger in Jesus' name.

THE BLESSING

May you enjoy divine support in a time like this Jesus' name.

THE INVITATION

If you haven't received Jesus as your Lord and Savior, pray this prayer now: ***Dear Jesus, I believe you are the Son of God and that you died for me. Come into my heart and make me a child of God. I now believe you are my Savior and confess you are my Lord. I'm born again and now a child of God. Glory to God!***

Please read Romans 10:9-10

Day 33

Keep Sowing Your Harvest Is Guaranteed

"He that goeth forth and weepeth, bearing precious seed, shall doubtless come again with rejoicing, bringing his sheaves with him." (Psalms 126:6)

The opening scripture above made us know that reaping is certain for the sower, no matter what, it also shows to us some of the conditions that the sower must met during the time of sowing and the time of reaping.

Sowing sometimes goes with weeping or tears, giving is not always easy or convenient but we must keep doing it. Sometimes it is a painful sacrifice

Look at this scripture in **Psalms 126:5** it says, *"They that sow in tears shall reap in joy."* Keep sowing no matter what, even when it goes with tears, just sow because you shall reap with joy. Sowing creates your harvest, don't stop sowing, and your harvest or reaping and receiving shall not stop. Hallelujah

Sowing should not be by force it should be a response to the Word of God. It should be by faith. **2 Corinthians 9:7** says; *"Every man according as he purposeth in his heart, so let him give; not grudgingly, or of necessity: for God loveth a cheerful giver."*

Learn to sow big according to what you have and can sacrifice. 2 **Corinthians 9:6** says, *"But this I say, He which soweth sparingly shall reap also sparingly; and he which soweth bountifully shall reap also bountifully."*

Remember your reaping is guaranteed. Don't stop giving, don't stop sowing at every opportunity.

Galatians 6:9-10, *"And let us not be weary in well doing: for in due season we shall reap, if we faint not. 6:10 As we have therefore opportunity, let us do good unto all men, especially unto*

them who are of the household of faith. " All the seeds that you've sowed these past years, (giving of your time, money, services, and the souls you won into the kingdom of God) shall provoke a harvest of rewards in due season. Don't stop sowing.

Let your desired harvest determine your seed always. Glory to God!

PRAYER

Father thank you for the life of faith you have called us into, by which we are living and excelling in every aspect of life. Today I am strengthened and energized to give again and again knowing fully well that my harvest is certain. Glory to you forever in Jesus' name.

THE BLESSING

May you encounter helpers of destiny today in Jesus' name. An increase of grace is your portion in life in Jesus' name.

THE INVITATION

If you haven't received Jesus as your Lord and Savior, pray this prayer now: ***Dear Lord Jesus, I believe you are the Son of God and that you died for my sins. Come into my heart and make me a child of God. I now receive you as my Savior and confess you as the Lord of my life. I am born again in Jesus' name. Glory!***

Please read, Romans 10:9-10

Day 34

Be Spiritually Minded

"For to be carnally minded is death; but to be spiritually minded is life and peace.

Because the carnal mind is enmity against God: for it is not subject to the law of God, neither indeed can be." (Romans 8:6-7)

God wants us to be spiritually minded as Christians according to the revelation in our opening scripture for today. If you read the entire book of Romans chapter eight you will see that much is said about today's topic.

The Bible says to be carnally minded is death, which means, a carnal mind produces death (sicknesses, poverty, fear, wrongdoings, failures, and destructions).

The will of God for us is life in abundance, Jesus came to give us life. The Bible says: ***"The thief cometh not, but for to steal, and to kill, and to destroy: I am come that they might have life, and that they might have it more abundantly." (John 10:10)***

Train yourself to be spiritually minded as a Christian, don't be carnally minded. You can't spend hours watching secular movies, enjoying the wrong company, listening to evil communications, etc: and be spiritually minded. There are things you must not do, there are places you must not go to. Remember as God's children, we are separated unto Him. We are not of this world. **1 John 2:15-16** tells us, ***"Love not the world, neither the things that are in the world. If any man loves the world, the love of the Father is not in him.***

2:16 For all that is in the world, the lust of the flesh, and the lust of the eyes, and the pride of life, is not of the Father, but is of the world."

Spend time in doing the things of God, such as reading the Bible, reading profitable and edifying books, praying for several minutes or hours.

Separate from the crowd to seek the Lord and you will see life flowing in you and through you, and your light shining brighter and brighter in the midst of the darkness of this world as God desires for you. **Philippians 2:15** says; "***That ye may be blameless and harmless, the sons of God, without rebuke, in the midst of a crooked and perverse nation, among whom ye shine as lights in the world;***"

Be God and righteousness conscious always. Glory to God!

It is me to be more spiritually minded and live victoriously in Christ in a time like this. **Philippians 3:15** says; "***Let us therefore, as many as be perfect, be thus minded: and if in anything ye be otherwise minded, God shall reveal even this unto you.***"

PRAYER

Father thank you for your word that is always available to guide us in our Christian life. As I walk in the light of your word today my light is shining brighter and brighter and I am moving from glory to glory in Jesus' name.

THE BLESSING

I pray this new month shall be for your good in Jesus' name. You will finish it stronger!

THE INVITATION

If you haven't received Jesus Christ as your Lord and Savior, pray this prayer now: ***Dear Lord Jesus, I believe you are the Son of God and that you died for my sins. Come into my heart and make me a child of God in Jesus' name. I now received you as my Lord and Savior. I am born again. Glory!***

Please read Romans 10:9-10

Day 35

Relax God Is Taking Care Of You

"Humble yourselves therefore under the mighty hand of God, that he may exalt you in due time:

Casting all your care upon him; for he careth for you." (1 Peter 5:6-7)

"For ye are dead, and your life is hid with Christ in God." (Colossians 3:3)

If you are born again you are a new creature, a child of the Almighty God and He is taking care of you. He is concern about you. He protects you from all evils. The very day you confessed Jesus as the Lord of your life he took over the lordship of your life. You are no longer yours but Christ's. Hallelujah!

Carefully study our opening scriptures for today. There are amazing.

Live joyfully, doing the word and work of God, telling the world about Jesus Christ, and bringing men to the knowledge of salvation by sharing or preaching the word of God to them and by the power of the Holy Ghost.

Always be conscious of this truth, God cares for you, and never become worried about your life anymore. Be conscious of the fact that you just have a beautiful life in Christ. Hallelujah!

The Bible says, "*And we know that all things work together for good to them that love God, to them who are the called according to his purpose. 8:29 For whom he did foreknow, he also did predestinate to be conformed to the image of his Son, that he might be the firstborn among many brethren. 8:30 Moreover whom he did predestinate, them he also called: and whom he called, them he also justified: and whom he justified, them he also glorified."* *Romans 8:28-30*. Glory to God!

The Bible says, "**And we know that all things work together for good to them that love God, to them who are the called according to his purpose. 8:29 For whom he did foreknow, he also did predestinate to be conformed to the image of his Son, that he might be the firstborn among many brethren.**

8:30 Moreover whom he did predestinate, them he also called: and whom he called, them he also justified: and whom he justified, them he also glorified." **Romans 8:28-30**. Glory to God!

As the world is going through this season of great danger, do not become worried about anything, but commit your life to him that is able to keep you until that day. Be watchful and prayerful as you listen to the Holy Spirit for directions and revelations from his word. Fear not, God is taking care of you.

PRAYER

Father thank you because you care for me, you are concerned about all that concerns me and you are perfecting them all in Jesus' name. I enjoy a worry-free life daily. My heart is full of joy and your joy is my strength. Hallelujah, Amen

THE BLESSING

May the grace of God keep you and your family safe from all evils in Jesus' name.

THE INVITATION

If you haven't received Jesus Christ as your Lord and Savior, pray this prayer now: *Dear Lord Jesus, I believe you are the Son of God and that you died for my sins. Come into my heart and make me a child of God in Jesus' name. I now received you as my Lord and Savior. I am born again. Glory!*

Please read Romans 10:9-10

Day 36

Heart Connection In Worship

"But the hour cometh, and now is, when the true worshippers shall worship the Father in spirit and in truth: for the Father seeketh such to worship him.

24 God is a Spirit: and they that worship him must worship him in spirit and in truth." (John 4:23-24)

There must be a connection between us and God in worship; because Christianity is a relationship with the Almighty God, it is not just a church activity but an expression of our relationship with God.

As Christians, it is expected that we get involved in some form of worship and another. We must pray, sing, give, evangelize, and do all we do for the Kingdom of God from our hearts. For effectiveness, we must connect with God in our spirits because God is a Spirit. (John 4:24).

He desires truth in the inward path, in the heart. **Psalms 51:6, "Behold, thou desirest truth in the inward parts: and in the hidden part thou shalt make me know wisdom."** The Bible says that the effective fervent prayer is the one that makes power available. **James 5:16, "Confess your faults one to another, and pray one for another, that ye may be healed. The effectual fervent prayer of a righteous man availeth much."**

When there is no connection with God in our spirit, all we have is mere religion. Remember Jesus's word to the people who worshipped with their mouths without the involvement of their hearts. Jesus rebuked them.

Please check your heart and consider your Christian activities and be sure there is a deeper connection with God in your heart. Whatever you are doing for the Lord be sure your heart is involved. **Ephesians 5:19,** "*Speaking to yourselves in psalms and hymns and spiritual songs, singing and making melody in your heart to the Lord.*"

PRAYER

Father thank you for the opportunity to be alive and to be in Christ. I live to worship you in all that I do for you and your Kingdom on earth in Jesus' name.

THE BLESSING

I pray you be will be enveloped and shielded from all evils in Jesus' name. Shine like a star!

THE INVITATION

If you haven't received Jesus Christ as your Lord and Savior, pray this prayer now*: **Dear Lord Jesus, I believe you are the Son of God and that you died for my sins. Come into my heart and make me a child of God. I now received you as my Savior and confess you as the Lord of my life. I am born again and now a child of God. Glory!***

Please read Romans 10:9-10

Day 37

Glory All The Way In Christ

"To whom God would make known what is the riches of the glory of this mystery among the Gentiles; which is Christ in you, the hope of glory." (Colossians 1:27)

The most important thing in life is Christ in you and you in Christ. This becomes a reality by faith, your believing in and receiving Jesus as your Savior and Lord make this possible.

John 1:12-13; *"But as many as received him, to them gave he power to become the sons of God, even to them that believe on his name:*

1:13 Which were born, not of blood, nor of the will of the flesh, nor of the will of man, but of God."

If you are in Christ and he is in you, there is a mysterious life of glory, a life of hope in every situation according to our opening scripture for today.

Remember God works in mysterious ways that man cannot understand nor predicted. He uses all things together for his children's good. **Romans 8:28** says; *"And we know that all things work together for good to them that love God, to them who are the called according to his purpose."*

God is God because he is able to do exceeding abundantly above all we ask or think. **Ephesians 3:20** says, *"Now unto him that is able to do exceeding abundantly above all that we ask or think, according to the power that worketh in us."*

No matter where you are or what you are going through right now, you are not for shame but glory.

Load yourself with the Word of God and let it be your constant confessions and meditations.

Say it out loud several times daily, *"I am for the glory of God and not for shame!"* And it shall manifest in your life. Glory!

Isaiah 60:1 says, "*Arise, shine; for thy light is come, and the glory of the LORD is risen upon thee. 60:2 For, behold, the darkness shall cover the earth, and gross darkness the people: but the LORD shall arise upon thee, and his glory shall be seen upon thee.*"

Rise in your spirit and begin to shine in the word by the power of the Holy Spirit. Glory to God!

PRAYER

Dear father, thank you very much for your grace and mercy. Today I declare by your word that my life is for your glory in Jesus' name. My light is shining brighter and brighter because your life is in me in Jesus' name. Hallelujah

THE BLESSING

May the power of his glory swallow up every shame and intended shame in your life in Jesus' name. Amen

THE INVITATION

If you haven't received Jesus Christ as your Lord and Savior, pray this prayer now: *Dear Lord Jesus, I believe you are the Son of God and that you died for my sins. Come into my heart and make me a child of God in Jesus' name. I now received you as my Lord and Savior. I am born again. Glory!*

Please read Romans 10:9-10

Day 38

Put Your Life In Order

"Let all things be done decently and in order." (1 Corinthians 14:40)

As God's children, because of our faith in the death, burial, and resurrection of Jesus Christ and by the confession of the Lordship of Jesus Christ over our life (**Romans 10:9-10**). We need to live in line with the Word of God so that we could enjoy the benefits of our salvation in Christ Jesus fully. One thing that is commanded by the Holy Spirit in our scriptural text for today is that all things must be done in order.

God believes in order and He is a God of order and not of confusion according to **1 Corinthians 14:33** that says; *"For God is not the author of confusion, but of peace, as in all churches of the saints."*

We as the children of God must be orderly in all that we do by putting our lives, activities, and things in proper order. This we can do by living according to the revelation and our conviction in the Word of God. Doing things disorderly causes, waste, confusion, stagnation, poverty, anger, and pains. When things are in order there is progress and peace naturally.

Some people spent so much money on unnecessary things because they are living out of order. Their marriages and families are in shambles because there is no order. Wherever there is disorderliness there are so many evils and pains.

Prayerfully plan and put your life in order today by the leading of the Holy Spirit and see how beautiful and peaceful your life can be. Ponder the path of thy feet, and let all thy ways be established. (**Proverbs 4:26**)

Apostle Paul said in **Colossians 2:5, *"For though I be absent in the flesh, yet am I with you in the spirit, joying and beholding your order, and the steadfastness of your faith in Christ."*** He also told Titus in **Titus 1:5,** "*For this cause left I thee in Crete, that thou shouldest set in order the things that are wanting, and ordain elders in every city, as I had appointed thee*:"

Sit down and think, prayerfully analyze your life, ask questions, where am I, why am I here, where am I heading to in life and how am I intending to get there? Have a plan of action or actions and stick to it. As you proceed, always depend on the Word of God and the Holy Spirit to lead and guide you through. You are succeeding in Jesus' name. Hallelujah!

If you belong to a group, family, or a local church, endeavor to follow instructions and directions by the leader to promote orderliness.

Orderliness is essential to success in life. Read the opening scripture for today again and meditate on it.

"***Let all things be done decently and in order***." (**1 Corinthians 14:40**)

PRAYER

Father thank You for Your Word and the Holy Spirit that is always available to guide us aright in life. I refuse to live disorderly but decently, orderly, and constructively in Jesus' name. Thank You, Father, that as I do this I gain speed in life and manifest your power, salvation, glory, and joy to others in the world around me in Jesus' name.

THE BLESSING

The grace for orderliness is operating in you in Jesus' name.

THE INVITATION

If you haven't received Jesus as your Lord and Savior, pray this prayer now: *Lord Jesus, I believe You are the Son of God, I believe that You died for my sins. Come into my heart and make me a child of God. I now receive you as my Savior and confess you as the Lord of my life in Jesus' name.*

Please Read Romans 10:9-10

Day 39

Train Yourself To Live Constructively Daily

"Watch and pray, that ye enter not into temptation: the spirit indeed is willing, but the flesh is weak." (Matthew 26:41)

Jesus said, ***"Watch and pray,"*** according to our opening scripture for today. This means that we are expected as believers in Jesus Christ to leave a constructive life, we are not allowed to live carelessly or disorderly but to live a life of watchfulness, organized and well-planned life, this is essential to avoid falling into avoidable troubles and ultimate failure.

Watchfulness could connote paying attention to details. For instance, some people only pray but lives carelessly and by so caused pains and sorrows for themselves and others contrary to the plan of God for their life. **1 Peter 5:8** says, "***Be sober, be vigilant; because your adversary the devil, as a roaring lion, walketh about, seeking whom he may devour.***"

Careless living is dangerous and can cause a whole lot of troubles, such as sin, sickness, poverty, anger, hunger, lack of personal growth and development, unnecessary pain and injuries, or may even lead to death etc.

Brethren let us heed the Master's command, he says, ***"WATCH AND PRAY THAT YE ENTER NOT INTO TEMPTATIONS"***

Watchfulness in every aspect of life shall preserve us from a whole lot of problems in this world. Hallelujah!

Ephesians 5:15 says, "***See then that ye walk circumspectly, not as fools, but as wise,***" No more foolishness, it is time for wisdom, paying attention and having a plan of action in every aspect of our lives to guide our activities.

Success comes only to those who engage themselves in an organized activity. Glory!

PRAYER

Dear Father, I give you all the glory for your commitment to our success in life. I received help by the anointing of the Holy Spirit to live soberly and to be watchful in Jesus' name. I am conscious of every step I am taking from this day forward in Jesus' name. I walk in wisdom and victory. Amen

THE BLESSING

I decree your glory shall not diminish in Jesus' name. Help is coming to you from unexpected sources in the name of the Lord Jesus Christ.

THE INVITATION

If you haven't received Jesus as your Savior and Lord, say this prayer now: *Dear Lord Jesus, I believe you are the Son of God and that you died for my sin. Come into my heart and make me a child of God. I now believe and confess you as the Lord of my life. I am born again and now a child of God. Hallelujah!*

Please read Romans 10:9-10

Day 40

Fight On To The End

"Fight the good fight of faith, lay hold on eternal life, whereunto thou art also called, and hast professed a good profession before many witnesses." (1 Timothy 6:12)

We are commanded by the Word of God to *"FIGHT THE GOOD FIGHT OF FAITH"* and *"LAY HOLD ON ETERNAL LIFE"* according to our opening scripture for today. This shows that we have the responsibility to fight the good fight of faith and to lay hold on eternal life always. We must keep our faith and always have heaven in view as we keep fighting until the end when we possess our possessions.

Don't give up your Christian faith, don't surrender to sin, don't embrace unrighteousness, don't allow depression or discouragement to stop you from believing, and from following the Lord Jesus Christ. Keep endeavoring to do the right thing, the word of God always by the power of the Holy Spirit.

Don't give up on your Godly and righteous dreams and goals. Put yourself together and do what it takes. Life could be tough sometimes, but as we put ourselves together and fight using the Word of God, prayer, and fasting, and by depending on the anointing of the Holy Spirit, difficult things will become easy and achievable.

Learn to be a tough fighter, Jesus says in **Matthew 11:12,** **"*And from the days of John the Baptist until now the kingdom of heaven suffereth violence, and the violent take it by force.*"**

Keep fighting, don't give up your faith. God's word can never fail. Study and meditate on the Word daily and keep moving on by the power of the Holy Spirit.

Never forget, YOU ARE BORN TO WIN IN CHRIST and you are always a winner no matter what.

Whatever you are going through today shall pass and you shall testify to the glory of God. Hallelujah!

PRAYER

Father thank you for your love and power that energizes me to never give up my faith in you. I am winning and winning in every aspect of life by the anointing of the Holy Spirit in Jesus' name. I am pressing daily towards the prize of the high calling in Christ Jesus in Jesus' name.

THE BLESSING

May today work for your favor in Jesus' name. May your wasted years be restored to you in Jesus' name.

THE INVITATION

If you haven't received Jesus as your Lord and Savior, pray this prayer now: ***Dear Lord Jesus, I believe you are the Son of God, and that you died for my sins. Come into my heart and make me a child of God as I received you now as my Savior and confess you as the Lord of my life. I am born again. Glory to God!***

Please read Romans 10:9-10

Day 41

We Are More Than Conquerors

"Nay, in all these things we are more than conquerors through him that loved us.

For I am persuaded, that neither death, nor life, nor angels, nor principalities, nor powers, nor things present, nor things to come,

Nor height, nor depth, nor any other creature, shall be able to separate us from the love of God, which is in Christ Jesus our Lord." (Romans 8:37-39)

As Christians, we've been made more than conquerors in Christ. Whatever is happening around us or in our lives today, we are all more than conquerors according to our opening scripture for today. Those problems and challenges are temporal, they are not real, they are nothing but a mirage. Hallelujah!

The Bible says in **Ephesians 1:3, "*Blessed be the God and Father of our Lord Jesus Christ, who hath blessed us with all spiritual blessings in heavenly places in Christ.*"** We are already blessed with all spiritual blessings in heavenly places in Christ. Remember we are heavenly citizens living in this world as His Ambassadors.

No matter what is happening in this world, we are always a winner and we can never be disadvantaged anymore, it must turn out for our good. **Romans 8:28-31** says, "***And we know that all things work together for good to them that love God, to them who are the called according to his purpose.***

8:29 For whom he did foreknow, he also did predestinate to be conformed to the image of his Son, that he might be the firstborn among many brethren. 8:30 Moreover whom he did predestinate, them he also called: and whom he called, them he also justified: and whom he justified, them he also glorified.

8:31 What shall we! Then say to these things? If God be for us, who can be against us?"

NO MATTER WHAT YOU ARE GOING THROUGH RIGHT NOW YOU ARE STILL MORE THAN CONQUEROR. Hallelujah!

Take your eyes off the problem. Soak yourself in the Word of God, meditate on it always, live by the word, and enjoy a wonderful kind of life.

Don't forget to pray in the tongues of the Holy Spirit open to make power available for the miraculous. Keep winning in life.

Remember you can never be defeated anymore, you are connected with God and his promises are yea and amen in Christ Jesus. Hallelujah!

PRAYER

Dear Father, what a glorious life we have in You, a life of more than a conqueror. Thank You for I can never be disadvantaged in life anymore because you are using all things together for my good in Jesus' name. My life is changing from glory to glory in Jesus' name.

THE BLESSING

May you be strengthened, energized, and empowered in the inner man in Jesus' name.

THE INVITATION

If you haven't received Jesus Christ as your Lord and Savior, pray this prayer now: ***Dear Lord Jesus, I believe you are the Son of God and that you died for my sins. Come into my heart and make me a child of God in Jesus' name. I now received you as my Savior and confess you as the Lord of my life. I am born again. Glory to God!***

Please read Romans 10:9-10

Day 42

Look Up To God

"I will lift up mine eyes unto the hills, from whence cometh my help.

My help cometh from the Lord, which made heaven and earth.

He will not suffer thy foot to be moved: he that keepeth thee will not slumber.

Behold, he that keepeth Israel shall neither slumber nor sleep.

The Lord is thy keeper: the Lord is thy shade upon thy right hand.

The sun shall not smite thee by day, nor the moon by night.

The Lord shall preserve thee from all evil: he shall preserve thy soul.

The Lord shall preserve thy going out and thy coming in from this time forth, and even for evermore." (Psalms 121:1-8)

Our opening scripture for today is loaded with revelations of who to look up to in life and why we must look up to God. We must look up to God because He can never fail no matter what. He is always powerful, without limitations. He is not careless but he's concern about us. He is able to do all things. He is stable. He is always the same yesterday, today, and forever. Nothing is too difficult for him. He has many ways to meet our needs. He uses all things together for our good.

Man may fail and will fail us, because of the limitations of man.

Man is here today and tomorrow he's gone. Man is strong right now and the next minutes he is weak. Look up to God in every situation and challenges of life; He knows just what to do. **Hebrews 12:2** says, "***Looking unto Jesus the author and finisher of our faith...***"

From this day let us keep (fix) our eyes on Jesus, He will never disappoint us in any way. Spend quality me to listen to Him daily in His words by reading, meditating on and hearing the Word of God from his servants. Spend quality time to fellowship and talk to Him in prayers

Trust Him absolutely. **Isaiah 2:22** says, "***Cease ye from man, whose breath is in his nostrils: for wherein is he to be accounted of?***"

Hebrews 12:2 also says, "***Looking unto Jesus the author and finisher of our faith; who for the joy that was set before him endured the cross, despising the shame, and is set down at the right hand of the throne of God.***"

Stop looking to man and start looking up to God, he will never disappoint you. Know and live by his divine instructions concerning every aspect of your life and see how your life will steadily move forward in every aspect by the power of the Holy Spirit. Glory to God!

PRAYER

Dear Father, I thank you this day for all you have done for us in Christ Jesus. As I set my eyes on you today, I experience peace and joy in Jesus' name. My progress is visible for all to see in Jesus' name. I am a success.

THE BLESSING

May all that rise against you fall for your sakes in Jesus' name. You shall excel today in Jesus' name.

THE INVITATION

If you haven't received Jesus as your Lord and Savior, pray this prayer now: ***Dear Lord Jesus, I believe you are the Son of God, and that you died for my sins. Come into my heart and make me a child of God as I now received you as my Savior and confess you as the Lord of my life. I am born again. Glory to God.***

Please read Romans 10:9-10

Day 43

Let The Word Of Christ Dwell In You Richly

"Let the word of Christ dwell in you richly in all wisdom; teaching and admonishing one another in psalms and hymns and spiritual songs, singing with grace in your hearts to the Lord." (Colossians 3:16)

The scripture above tells us what should dwell or occupy our mind and spirit, it is THE WORD OF CHRIST.

As a Christian, we must endeavor to know the word; we must consciously load ourselves with the word of Christ daily.

Words are very powerful, the words that occupy our minds is what will determine our actions and our behaviors. If we desire to walk in newness of life, then we must load ourselves with the word of God. Make reading, hearing, and meditating the Word of God your incurable habit.

The book of **Joshua 1:8** says, "*This book of the law shall not depart out of thy mouth; but thou shalt meditate therein day and night, that thou mayest observe to do according to all that is written therein: for then thou shalt make thy way prosperous, and then thou shalt have good success.*"

Remember again that **Colossians 3:16** tells us that the word will make us have all wisdom, and also help us to teach and admonish one another. It is a beautiful thing when believers come together sharing the Scriptures.

The world talks about what filled their hearts. We must think and talk the word of God. It must not depart out of our mouth and our mind. Our actions must be based on the Word of God.

The Holy Spirit is always there to remind us what we have learned; we can depend on Him to help us remember the Word of God.

Get serious with the word of Christ now that you are in Him.

1 Peter 2:2-3 says, "*As newborn babes, desire the sincere milk of the word, that ye may grow thereby: 2:3 If so be ye have tasted that the Lord is gracious.*"

The word in you will determine how strong you are in Christ and how much your life is conformed to the word of God and how many exploits you will do.

PRAYER

Father, I thank you today for the light of your word that is lighting my path. I received grace to load myself with your word in Jesus' name. Father, your word the Bible is very alive to me afresh as I study, hear and meditate in it in Jesus' name.

THE BLESSING

May the doors of unusual breakthrough open up for you this month of beauty in Jesus' name.

INVITATION

If you haven't received Jesus as your Savior, pray this prayer now: **Lord Jesus, I believe that you are the Son of God and that you died for my sins. Come into my heart and make me a child of God. I now believe you are my Savior and confess you as the Lord of my life. I am born again. Hallelujah!**

Please read Romans 10:9-10

Day 44

Observe To Do All Things For A Balance Living

"Teaching them to observe all things whatsoever I have commanded you: and, lo, I am with you always, even unto the end of the world. Amen." (Matthew 28:20)

My emphasis from today's opening scripture is "OBSERVE ALL THINGS" because there is a need for us to live a balanced life as Christians. Jesus was saying to his disciples, teach people to observe all things that he commanded the Apostles as believers in Christ.

We must endeavor to give attention to every aspect of our life. God is not a one-sided God but the God of order and He expects His children to be orderly just like him. Read Genesis chapter one and see the account of creation to see how orderly God is.

Apostle Paul by the Holy Spirit told Timothy in **2 Timothy 2:15, "*Study to shew thyself approved unto God, a workman that needeth not to be ashamed, rightly dividing the word of truth.*"** *"RIGHTLY DIVIDING THE WORD OF TRUTH!"* We must endeavor to live a balanced life, applying the word of truth in every aspect of life as this scripture has taught us.

In order to live a balanced life, one must have proper all-round spiritual development of oneself. He must get basic information about life and things necessary in the Bible and good books, so as to be able to live a balanced and constructive life.

Any area we do not pay attention to becomes a breeding ground for the devil and avoidable problems. Give no place, no chance to the devil to operate in your life. The Bible says in **Ephesians 4:27, "*Neither give place to the devil.*"**

Please begin to live a balanced life now. Don't overdo anything at the expense of another, attend to all that is necessary for your life on a daily, weekly, monthly, or yearly basis. Hallelujah!

PRAYER

Father thank you in the name of the Lord Jesus Christ. I receive grace and wisdom to live a balanced life from this day forward in Jesus' name. I give no room to the devil in any aspect of my life. My life is orderly and peaceful in Jesus' name.

THE BLESSING

Receive the necessary grace now in Jesus' name. As you desire it, receive it in Jesus' name. You are a winner.

THE INVITATION

If you haven't received Jesus as your Lord and Savior, pray this prayer now: ***Lord Jesus, I believe you are the Son of God and that you died for my sins. Come into my heart and make me a child of God. I now confess you as my Lord and Savior. I am born again, a child of God. In Jesus' name.***

Please read Romans 10:9-10

Day 45

Stir Up Yourself To Action

"Wherefore I put thee in remembrance that thou stir up the gift of God, which is in thee by the putting on of my hands." (2 Timothy 1:6)

The opening scripture above tells us of the instruction of the great Apostle Paul to Timothy his son in the faith. He told him to stir up the gift of God in him.

As believers in Jesus Christ, we must learn how to stir up our faith, our gift, and ourselves. This means we must do something that can spur us to action all the time. Many times, one may be too cold, sluggish and lazy, or careless, and this may render one's gift or ability useless. There are lots we can do as children of God but it may not happen until we learn how to stir up ourselves.

The Bible shows us that praying in the Holy Ghost can build up or stir us up within on our most holy faith. **Jude 1:20** says, **"*But ye, beloved, building up yourselves on the most holy faith, praying in the Holy Ghost*."** Use praying in tongues to charge yourself. Use listening to the teachings of the word to charge yourself. Use praise and worship (personal and on tapes) to charge yourself.

We have to devise means of self-motivation in prayers, fasting, service, soul-winning, and in doing all that is expected of us in every aspect of life, this will make us a living and a winning Christian in life. Start today.

Be conscious of who you are and your assignments in life as a Christian and begin to do what is expected of you with little or no external push or pressure. **Isaiah 60:1** says, **"*Arise, shine; for thy light is come, and the glory of the LORD is risen upon thee.*"** Glory to God!

PRAYER

Father thank you for the divine ability that is in me to do exploits in life. Today I ginger myself by the power of the Holy Spirit to do your word in Jesus' name. I function in my place and enjoy peace, joy, and progress supernaturally today in Jesus' name.

THE BLESSING

May grace announce you from this day forward in Jesus' name. Every demonic weakness is removed out of your life now in Jesus' name.

THE INVITATION

If you haven't received Jesus as your Lord and Savior, pray now: ***Dear Lord Jesus, I believe you are the son of God and that you died for my sins, come into my heart, and make me a child of God. I now receive you as my savior and confess you as the Lord of my life, I am born again. Glory to God***

Please read Romans 10:9-10

Day 46

Power To Effect Changes

"Confess to one another therefore your faults (your slips, your false steps, your offenses, your sins) and pray [also] for one another, that you may be healed and restored [to a spiritual tone of mind and heart]. The earnest (heartfelt, continued) prayer of a righteous man makes tremendous power available [dynamic in its working]." (James 5:16 AMPC)

As a Christian, there comes a time when there are situations that needed to change in order to avoid some unfavorable conditions in every aspect of your life. Apart from the faith which is fundamental to our Christian life, there is one thing that can always bring a change to any situation in life, it is the power of the Spirit of God made available by prayers.

If you can pray, things will change. God said in **Jeremiah 33:3,** *"Call unto me, and I will answer thee, and shew thee great and mighty things, which thou knowest not."*

For instance, the Bible testified that Jabez became fed up with his situation, he called upon God and he answered him. *"**And Jabez was more honorable than his brethren: and his mother called his name Jabez, saying, Because I bare him with sorrow. 4:10 And Jabez called on the God of Israel, saying, oh that thou wouldest bless me indeed, and enlarge my coast, and that thine hand might be with me, and that thou wouldest keep me from evil, that it may not grieve me! And God granted him that which he requested."* **(1 Chronicles 4:9-10)**

You must know the Word of God and learn how to call upon God in prayers by yourself because this will help you develop a personal relationship with God and you will be able to call him FATHER.

Matthew 6:9 says, *"**After this manner therefore pray ye: Our Father which art in heaven, Hallowed be thy name."*

The Bible says your prayer as a Christian is able to make power to cause a change you desire available according to our opening scripture for today, read also in KJV it says, "***Confess your faults one to another, and pray one for another, that ye may be healed. The effectual fervent prayer of a righteous man availeth much.***" **(James 5:16)**

Are there situations that need to change, begin to pray especially in tongues for a long me consistently and you will see great and mighty things happening in your life and the world around you by the power of the Holy Spirit that you are making available through prayers.

Get the word of God concerning your need and your desire, set your heart, and pray all manners of prayers about it. Pray especially in the tongues of the Holy Spirit. It works!

Use the opportunity you have right now in a time like this to pray fervently in tongues and understanding. Something is happening as you pray, you are making power available.

PRAYER

Father thank you for the line of relationship, communication, and connection with you you've made available for me to constantly use for a life of miracle signs and wonders in Christ Jesus. As I make power available my life is moving forward from glory to glory in Jesus' name.

THE BLESSING

May you experience his greater glory in your life in Jesus' name.

THE INVITATION

If you haven't received Jesus Christ as your Lord and Savior, pray this prayer now: ***Dear Lord Jesus, I believe you are the Son of God and that you died for my sins. Come into my heart and make me a child of God in Jesus name. I now received you as my Lord and Savior. I am born again. Glory!***

Please read Romans 10:9-10

Day 47

Pray Until Something Happens

"And he spake a parable unto them to this end, that men ought always to pray, and not to faint;

Saying, There was in a city a judge, which feared not God, neither regarded man:

And there was a widow in that city; and she came unto him, saying, Avenge me of mine adversary.

And he would not for a while: but afterward he said within himself, Though I fear not God, nor regard man;

Yet because this widow troubleth me, I will avenge her, lest by her continual coming she weary me.

And the Lord said, Hear what the unjust judge saith.

And shall not God avenge his own elect, which cry day and night unto him, though he bear long with them?

I tell you that he will avenge them speedily. Nevertheless when the Son of man cometh, shall he find faith on the earth?" (Luke 18:1-8)

The portion of the scripture above tells us a beautiful story of a widow that was having a problem and a wicked Judge who neither fears God nor respects men. The woman in question continued to tell the Judge her problem and asking for his intervention. Jesus said, though the Judge refused to answer her at first, he eventually listened and did as the widow requested of him.

Jesus said, look at what the unjust Judge did because of the woman's consistency in asking the judge to avenged her, he answered her. Jesus taught us a great lesson there. WE MUST PRAY UNTIL SOMETHING HAPPENS or until we receive what we are asking for.

Never give up on praying. Pray continually. The answer is sure if you do not up. Hallelujah!

Remember your prayer works as a righteous child of God.

James 5:16 says, "***Confess your faults one to another, and pray one for another, that ye may be healed. The effectual fervent prayer of a righteous man availeth much***."

Go ahead and pray now, pray, again and again, pray all kinds of prayers in tongues and understanding based on the Word of God until you will receive. The answer is sure; you will have a miraculous life in Christ. Hallelujah! **Ephesians 6:18** says, "***Praying always with all prayer and supplication in the Spirit, and watching thereunto with all perseverance and supplication for all saints***."

Don't stop praying in a time like this. What an opportunity to pray long. Use it brother, use it, sister, don't let it be wasted by play, pleasure, and fun. You must achieve something great in a time like this. Glory to God!

PRAYER

Dear Father, I thank you once more for waking me up to see the light of a new day and for the new opportunities to live and make things happen. I receive an increase of grace to pray a heartfelt prayers until I receive answers that I desired in Jesus name.

THE BLESSING

I invoke on you God's divine ability today in Jesus' name.

THE INVITATION

If you haven't received Jesus Christ as your Lord and Savior, pray this prayer now: *Lord Jesus, I believe you are the Son of God and that you died for my sins. Come into my heart and make me a child of God. Amen.*

Please read Romans 10:9-10.

Day 48

Examine Yourself Whether You Be In The Faith

"Examine yourselves, whether ye be in the faith; prove your own selves. Know ye not your own selves, how that Jesus Christ is in you, except ye be reprobates?" (2 Corinthians 13:5)

As Christians, we are expected to search and examine ourselves according to our opening scripture for today, because faith is personal and it's of the heart.

Examining ourselves will help us to know what we are doing right or wrong and to be able to make amend where necessary. It will help us to become better and to grow without any external pressure from man.

When one fails to examine himself, he may fall into many errors or become fake or a hypocrite. We must constantly examine ourselves using the Word of God as the instrument of measurement.

Self-examination will help one to know his area of strength and weakness, as this will help in le ng others help in the area of weakness and to maximize one's strength.

When we examine ourselves we are allowing the Holy Spirit to work with us and make us see our true pictures and how we can change and become better in life.

Examine yourself now, make amend where necessary, and keep growing in the Lord. Always spend quality time to study and to meditate on the word of God personally and you will discover the areas you need to grow in your Christian life.

Examine yourself now, make amend where necessary, and keep growing in the Lord. Always spend quality time to study and to meditate on the Word of God personally and you will discover the areas you need to grow in your Christian life. Please read **2 Peter 1:5-10, "*And beside this, giving all diligence, add to your faith virtue; and to virtue knowledge; 1:6 And to*** *knowledge temperance; and to temperance patience; and to patience godliness; 1:7 And to godliness brotherly kindness; and to brotherly kindness charity. 1:8 For if these things be in you, and abound, they make you that ye shall neither be barren nor unfruitful in the knowledge of our Lord Jesus Christ.*

1:9 But he that lacketh these things is blind, and cannot see afar off, and hath forgotten that he was purged from his old sins. 1:10 Wherefore the rather, brethren, give diligence to make your calling and election sure: for if ye do these things, ye shall never fall."

PRAYER

Father you have given us the opportunity to build up ourselves on our most holy faith, today I acknowledge my faith in you and ready to keep growing in the faith so that I can continue to do exploits for your kingdom in Jesus' name. Amen

THE BLESSING

May the peace of the Lord preserve your heart and mind today in Jesus' name.

THE INVITATION

If you haven't received Jesus as your Lord and Savior, say this prayer now: **Lord Jesus, I believe you are the Son of God and that you died for my sins. Come into my heart and make me a child of God. I believe and confess you now as my Savior and the Lord of my life. I am now born again and a child of God. Glory to God!**

Please read Romans10:9-10

Day 49

When Praying In Tongues Is In Place

"Confess your faults one to another, and pray one for another, that ye may be healed. The effectual fervent prayer of a righteous man availeth much." (James 5:16)

"For he that speaketh in an unknown tongue speaketh not unto men, but unto God: for no man understandeth him; howbeit in the spirit he speaketh mysteries." (1 Corinthians 14:2)

According to the second part of the first scriptural text above, *"The effectual, fervent prayer of a righteous man avails much."* The second text also tells us what happened when we pray in tongues. Your prayer works. As Christians therefore we need to pray especially in tongues if we are going to see the great changes we desire by the power of the Holy Ghost.

What the Bible says about praying in tongues.

Romans 8:26, *"Likewise the Spirit also helpeth our infirmities: for we know not what we should pray for as we ought: but the Spirit itself maketh intercession for us with groanings which cannot be uttered."*

 The Holy Spirit helps us in praying the right way.

1 Corinthians 14:1, *"For if I pray in an unknown tongue, my spirit prayeth, but my understanding is unfruitful. Our spirit prays*.

1 Corinthians 14:4, *"He that speaketh in an unknown tongue edifieth himself; but he that prophesieth edifieth the church."*

We are edified.

Jude 1:20, *"But ye, beloved, building up yourselves on your most holy faith…"* praying in the Holy Ghost, there is building up.

In summary, when praying in tongues is in place. There will be rampant miracles, testimonies, fruitfulness, open doors, growth, increase, and building up.

TO PRAY IN TONGUES

Be born again

Receive and be filled with the Holy Spirit

Desire to pray in tongues

Practice praying in tongues always and grow in it.

Remember it is you who will speak in tongues as the Holy Spirit prompts you on the inside. Hallelujah! Make good use of this provision in a time like this and make mysterious living, progress, and grace available for yourself and others. Glory to God!

PRAYER

Dear Father, I thank you because of who you are and for the wonderful provision of prayers. As I pray I make power available for a change that I desire in the name of the Lord Jesus Christ.

THE BLESSING

I pray for you today, your appointment with failure is terminated in Jesus' name.

THE INVITATION

If you haven't received Jesus as your Lord and personal Savior, pray this prayer now: ***Dear Lord Jesus, I believe you are the Son of God and that you died for my sins. Come into my heart and*** *make me a child of God. I now receive you as my Savior and confess you as the Lord of my life.*

I am born again. Glory to God! Amen.

Please read Romans 10:9-10

Day 50

Opportunities And You

"To everything there is a season, and a time to every purpose under the heaven." (Ecclesiastes 3:1)

In life there are opportunities and one must understand some things about these opportunities of life, most especially as children of God so as to use them for our advantage and progress in life.

Our opening scripture for today says: *"To everything there is a season, and a time to every purpose under the heaven."* (Ecclesiastes 3:1)

Opportunities are the special message and seasons that come to a man to change his life for good.

It can come in the form of a relationship, business, information, academic, and even spiritual open doors or programs. What we do with those special seasons or me of life (opportunities) determines the next level or levels of our life.

You must make good use of opportunities that come your way. Don't throw them away, don't misuse or miss it.

You can quickly ask yourself these three questions:
How will this opportunity glorify God?
How will it bless others?
How will it change my life for the better?

If the answers to these questions are in the affirmative, go ahead, and do what it takes.

Every opportunity comes with a price tag and each me we missed it and it comes around again, the price goes up.

We must therefore learn to use opportunities the first me they come because the Bible says: *"Now is the day of salvation."* **2 Corinthians 6:1-2** says, **"*We then, as workers together with him, beseech you also that ye receive not the grace of God in vain. 6:2 (For he saith, I have heard thee in a time accepted, and in the day of salvation have I succored thee: behold, now is the accepted me; behold, now is the day of salvation.)*"**

The year 2021 is full of opportunities, be prayerful and watchful enough to discover and to make good use of the opportunities as it comes your way and you will become better and better in Jesus' name. Don't forget to depend on the Holy Spirit for divine directions concerning opportunities available when you are praying and studying the Word of God.

Be quick to notice and discover opportunities of life and use them for your advancement (financially, spiritually, academically, and socially) in life.

PRAYER
Father, I thank you for the opportunities you've made available for me in life. I receive grace to recognize and to use correctly every opportunity that will come my way from this day in Jesus' name.

THE BLESSING
May the Lord God Almighty preserve you from all evils in Jesus' name. Move to your next level of glory in Jesus' name.

THE INVITATION

If you haven't received Jesus as your Lord and Savior, pray from your heart now: ***Dear Lord Jesus, I believe you are the Son of God and that you died for my sins. Come into my heart and make me a child of God. I now receive you as my Savior and confess you as the Lord of my life. I am born again. Glory to God!***

Please Read. Romans 10:9-10

Day 51

Go For The Word Of God

"Only be thou strong and very courageous, that thou mayest observe to do according to all the law, which Moses my servant commanded thee: turn not from it to the right hand or to the left, that thou mayest prosper whithersoever thou goest.

This book of the law shall not depart out of thy mouth; but thou shalt meditate therein day and night, that thou mayest observe to do according to all that is written therein: for then thou shalt make thy way prosperous, and then thou shalt have good success." (Joshua 1:7-8)

As a child of God, you need revelations or understanding of how things work in the Kingdom of God, so that you can live and function to the glory of God and have good success in life. Jesus expects us to function by the word, in **Matthew 7:24** he said, "*Therefore whosoever heareth these sayings of mine, and doeth them, I will liken him unto a wise man, which built his house upon a rock:*"

In our opening scripture for today, God showed Joshua how to succeed in life, the word must always be in his mouth, he must meditate in it day and night, and he must observe to do all that is written in it. This is applicable to all of us today who believed and desire to prosper and have good success in Christ.

Like Joshua, if you want to succeed in life, go for the Word of God. Know the word for yourself, listen to the word open, spend quality time daily to study, and meditate continually in it. Get a jotter to jot the teachings of your man of God down so that you can go through it again and again until it becomes a total part of you and you are living by it. Don't treat the Word of God casually but be serious with it as a Christian.

Observe and consciously do all that is written and expected of you in the word and you shall be prosperous and have good success in life.

James 1:25, says, "*But whoso looketh into the perfect law of liberty, and continueth therein, he being not a forgetful hearer, but a doer of the work, this man shall be blessed in his deed.*" You must endeavor to do everything possible to know the Word of God and to do the word. All you need is in the Word of God. Go for the word. Glory to God!

Don't forget this, if you want to prosper and have good success in life, go for the Word of God. Know and live to practice the word and you will have glorious testimonies by the power of the Holy Ghost.

PRAYER

Father thank you for your constant leading and revelations of your word to me by which I rule and reign in this present world in the name of the Lord Jesus Christ. By your word I live victoriously, succeeding in all my endeavors in Jesus' name.

THE BLESSING

I decree and declare you shall excel in life in Jesus' name.

THE INVITATION

If you haven't received Jesus Christ as your Lord and Savior, pray this prayer now: ***Dear Lord Jesus, I believe you are the Son of God and that you died for my sins. Come into my heart and make me a child of God in Jesus' name. I now received you as my Lord and Savior. I am born again. Glory!***

Please read Romans 10:9-10

Day 52

Be Established In The Truth

"Be not carried about with divers and strange doctrines. For it is a good thing that the heart be established with grace; not with meats, which have not profited them that have been occupied therein." (Hebrews 13:9)

"The eyes of your understanding being enlightened; that ye may know what is the hope of his calling, and what the riches of the glory of his inheritance in the saints." (Ephesians 1:18)

As Christians, we are expected to be established in the truth according to our opening scriptures for today. There are those who are here and there, it is dangerous and damaging because it shows a lack of focus and strain forwardness in life, and they may find it difficult to excel in life. **Genesis 49:4** says, *"Unstable as water, thou shalt not excel ..."*

When one is not established, he will always be pushed to and fro by every wind of doctrines and by what people say, right or wrong. The Bible says in **Ephesians 4:12-14,** *"For the perfecting of the saints, for the work of the ministry, for the edifying of the body of Christ: 4:13 Till we all come in the unity of the faith, and of the knowledge of the Son of God, unto a perfect man, unto the measure of the stature of the fullness of Christ: 4:14 That we henceforth be no more children, tossed to and fro, and carried about with every wind of doctrine, by the sleight of men, and cunning craziness, whereby they lie in wait to deceive."*

Establishing on the truth brings stability and prosperity. It builds a strong and stable relationship. It builds a lasting business and makes money or profits making come easily. It aids understanding, as one will know how to use newly discovered truths or information correctly. When you know what to do you are free from confusion and time wasting most especially when you are a doer of the work thereof.

To be established in the truth, you need to know the word of God personally, you need to read profitable books for understanding.

Proper upbringing will also help children to have basic information that will serve as a platform for establishments in their lives. **Proverbs 22:6** says, "***Train up a child in the way he should go: and when he is old, he will not depart from it.***"

Pastors should endeavor to teach every convert or new people in the church in order for them to have a strong biblical foundation. Jesus says in **Matthew 28:19-20,** "***Go ye therefore, and teach all nations, baptizing them in the name of the Father, and of the Son, and of the Holy Ghost: 28:20 Teaching them to observe all things whatsoever I have commanded you: and, lo, I am with you always, even unto the end of the world. Amen***."

Remember that the Word of God is stable, build your life on it. Glory to God.

PRAYER

Father thank you for the opportunity to study your word always and for understanding by the help of the Holy Spirit. My heart is established by the truth in your word, I am excelling in every aspect of life in Christ Jesus. Amen

THE BLESSING

I pray today that God will establish you in life in Jesus' name.

THE INVITATION

If you haven't received Jesus Christ as your Lord and Savior, pray this prayer now*: **Dear Lord Jesus, I believe you are the Son of God and that you died for my sins. Come into my heart and make me a child of God. I now receive you as my Lord and Savior. I am born again. Glory!***

Please read Romans 10:9-10

Day 53

Build Your Faith Strong To Work For You

"So then faith cometh by hearing, and hearing by the word of God."
(Romans 10:17)

As God's children by faith in the Lord Jesus Christ, we have a measure of faith given to us by God in our hearts according to **Romans 12:3, *"For I say, through the grace given unto me, to every man that is among you, not to think of himself more highly than he ought to think; but to think soberly, according as God hath dealt to every man the measure of faith."***

The opening scripture for today says that faith cometh by hearing the Word of God. Our faith must be fed to keep it strong, healthy, and active. Faith without works (corresponding actions) is dead according to **James 2:26 "*For as the body without the spirit is dead, so faith without works is dead also*."**

To keep our faith alive, strong, and active, it is absolutely necessary to keep feeding it with the Word of God.
We must read and read the word of God again and again. Hear the word of God again and again. The book of **Romans 10:17** says: "*So then faith cometh by hearing, and hearing by the word of God.*"

As we go on in the year and in this trying period in the world, gather all the necessary materials needed, materials such as Christian's books, messages, CDs, DVDs, etc., and start using them.
Go to Church to listen to the preaching and teaching of the word of God by your man of God. Write down the messages in your jotter or notebook. Return home to read through again and meditate on the word so that you can become a doer of it.

(Joshua 1:8). Have devotional materials you can use daily and quality time set aside to seriously study, meditate on the word, and pray. There is much you can do or achieve with your faith in life if you feed: and build it strong. Jesus revealed what you should do with your faith and what your faith would do for you in **Mark 16:17-18, "*And these signs shall follow them that believe; In my name shall they cast out devils; they shall speak with new tongues; 16:18 They shall take up serpents; and if they drink any deadly thing, it shall not hurt them; they shall lay hands on the sick, and they shall recover.*"** Don't settle for less.

It is time to begin to feed the measure (seed) of faith that made you believed and received Jesus as Savior and Lord of your life in the first place with more of the word of God. The quality of your faith will determine the quality of the life you live.

PRAYER

Dear Father, I thank you once more for your word. As I feed my faith by reading and meditating in your word, my faith is growing stronger and stronger, increasing and increasing in Jesus' name. I do exploits this day for this is my day in Jesus' name. Hallelujah.

THE BLESSING

May your faith grow stronger and stronger to enjoy daily victory in Jesus' name.

THE INVITATION

If you haven't received Jesus as your Lord and Savior, say this prayer now: ***Lord Jesus, I believe you are the Son of God and that you died for my sins. Come into my heart and make me a child of God. I now receive you as my Savior and confess you as the Lord of my life. I am born again. Glory!***

Please read Romans 10:9-10

Day 54

Pray Immediately You Are Prompted To Pray

"Rejoicing in hope; patient in tribulation; continuing instant in prayer." (Romans 12:12)

Among the instructions to the churches in Rome by the Holy Spirit through Apostle Paul in the opening scripture above is that they should CONTINUE INSTANT IN PRAYERS. This means they don't have to keep prayer requests, prayer meeting time or the hour of prayers or until they are on the prayer mountain, but they are to respond to the inner prompt immediately they are moved to pray in their heart.

As the Holy Spirit prompts us to pray, we should start to pray immediately and waste no further time at all. To make this possible the Holy Spirit has given us all manners, forms, and patterns of prayers that we can always use when there is a need to pray.

Ephesians 6:18 says "*Praying always with all prayer and supplication in the Spirit, and watching thereunto with all perseverance and supplication for all saints.*"

We can pray in understanding. We can pray in the Holy Ghost.

 Jude 1:20, "*But ye, beloved, building up yourselves on your most holy faith, praying in the Holy Ghost.*"

We can pray in tongues.

1 Corinthians 14:4, "*He that speaketh in an unknown tongue edifieth himself; but he that prophesieth edifieth the church.*"

The conclusion of the message is, CONTINUE INSTANT IN PRAYERS. Learn to pray immediately you are prompted to pray about a thing, somebody, or a situation, it will save and deliver you from lots of troubles and help you to avoid the avoidable calamities in life.

Key into this great grace as a child of God and be instant in prayers don't wait until you get to Church fellowship before you pray. Pray instantly. **Luke 18:1** *".... men ought always to pray, and not to faint."*

PRAYER

Dear Father thank you for the grace of prayers, I received help to be sensitive to the Holy Spirit prompt always so that I can continue instant in prayers in Jesus name. As I pray I receive the answer according to your word in Jesus' name.

THE BLESSING

May you see great and mighty things that you know not in the remaining days of this year in Jesus' name.

THE INVITATION

If you have not received Jesus as your Lord and Savior, say this prayer now: *Dear Lord Jesus, I believe you are the Son of God and that you died for my sins. Come into my heart and make me a child of God. I now receive you as my Savior and confess you as the Lord of my life. I am born again. Amen.*

Please read Romans 10:9-10.

Day 55

Pray On Behalf Of Others

"Wherefore I also, after I heard of your faith in the Lord Jesus, and love unto all the saints,
Cease not to give thanks for you, making mention of you in my prayers." (Ephesians 1:15-16)

As Christians we need to pray for others, making mention of them in our prayers in these challenging times. We ought to have a list of people's names that we intercede for daily, this will go a long way to bless and help them. Our prayers can deliver them; it can make tremendous power available for a change in their life. Paul the apostle in our opening scripture for today said he prayed for the Ephesians church making mention of them.

If we read further, we can see the content of his prayers for the people, **Ephesians 1:16-19,** *"Cease not to give thanks for you, making men on of you in my prayers; 1:17 That the God of our Lord Jesus Christ, the Father of glory, may give unto you the spirit of wisdom and revelation in the knowledge of him: 1:18 The eyes of your understanding being enlightened; that ye may know what is the hope of his calling, and what the riches of the glory of his inheritance in the saints,*
1:19 And what is the exceeding greatness of his power to us-ward who believe, according to the working of his mighty power."

We can pray the same prayers for the brethren today. We must also pray for those in government so that they can rule (legislate and govern) in the fear of God. Read **1Timothy 2:1-3**: *"I exhort therefore, that, first of all, supplications, prayers, intercessions, and giving of thanks, be made for all men; 2:2 For kings, and for all that are in authority; that we may lead a quiet and peaceable life in all godliness and honesty."*

If they make wrong decisions, it will affect everybody including the Church. We must intercede for the salvation of sinners that the gospel will penetrate their hearts. We can intercede for the outpouring of the Holy Spirit upon our nation and the world.

Let us wake up to our responsibility of interceding for our brothers and sisters, relations, nations, and our world and especially for the believers in a time like this. Hallelujah!

PRAYER

Father thank you for every opportunity you gave us to function as a Christian. Let the spirit of intercession come upon me today in Jesus' name. Forgive me for my failure to intercede for others in the past in Jesus' name.

THE BLESSING

I pray God's grace will increase in your life today in Jesus' name. I pray you will be delivered from the hand of the wicked and the unreasonable men in Jesus' name.

THE INVITATION

If you haven't received Jesus as Savior and Lord, pray this prayer now: ***Dear Lord Jesus, I believe you are the Son of God and that you died for my sins. Come into my heart and make me a child of God. I now believe and confess Jesus as my Savior and Lord of my life. I am born again in Jesus' name.***

Read Romans 10:9-10

Day 56

Glory All The Way In Christ

"To whom God would make known what is the riches of the glory of this mystery among the Gentiles; which is Christ in you, the hope of glory." (Colossians 1:27)

The most important thing in life is Christ in you and you in Christ. This becomes a reality by faith, your believing in and receiving Jesus as your Savior and Lord make this possible.

John 1:12-13: "*But as many as received him, to them gave he power to become the sons of God, even to them that believe on his name: 1:13 Which were born, not of blood, nor of the will of the flesh, nor of the will of man, but of God.*"

If you are in Christ and he is in you, there is a mysterious life of glory, a life of hope in every situation of life according to our opening scripture for today.

Remember God works in mysterious ways that man cannot understand nor predicted. He uses all things together for his children's good. **Romans 8:28** says: *"And we know that all things work together for good to them that love God, to them who are the called according to his purpose."*

God is God because he is able to do exceeding abundantly above all we ask or think. **Ephesians 3:20** says: *"Now unto him that is able to do exceeding abundantly above all that we ask or think, according to the power that worketh in us."*

No matter where you are or what you are going through right now, you are not for shame but glory. Load yourself with the Word of God and let it be your constant confessions and meditations.

Say it out loud several times daily, *"I am for the glory of God and not for shame!"* And it shall manifest in your life. Glory!

Isaiah 60:1-2 says: "*Arise, shine; for thy light is come, and the glory of the LORD is risen upon thee. 60:2 For, behold, the darkness shall cover the earth, and gross darkness the people: but the LORD shall arise upon thee, and his glory shall be seen upon thee.*" Rise up in your spirit and begin to shine in the world by the power of the Holy Spirit. Shout, Glory to God!

PRAYER

Dear father, thank you very much for your grace and mercy. Today I declare by your word that my life is for your glory in Jesus' name. My light is shining brighter and brighter because your life is in me in Jesus' name. Hallelujah

THE BLESSINGS

May the power of his glory swallow up every shame and intended shame in your life in Jesus' name. Amen

THE INVITATION

If you haven't received Jesus Christ as your Lord and Savior, pray this prayer now: *Dear Lord Jesus, I believe you are the Son of God and that you died for my sins. Come into my heart and make me a child of God in Jesus' name. I now received you as my Lord and Savior. I am born again. Glory!*

Please read Romans 10:9-10

Day 57

Apply The Word To Every Aspect Of Your Life

"And it shall come to pass, if thou shalt hearken diligently unto the voice of the Lord thy God, to observe and to do all his commandments which I command thee this day, that the Lord thy God will set thee on high above all nations of the earth:
And all these blessings shall come on thee, and overtake thee, if thou shalt hearken unto the voice of the Lord thy God." (Deuteronomy 28:1-2)

As children of God, it is expected of us by God to live by His word. In the Old Testament, he gave the Israelites commandments, set of rules by the hand of his prophets to guide their conduct. He was concerned about every aspect of their lives and made provisions for all aspects of his commandments. There were the Ten Commandments and many other instructions, the purpose of all was to make sure they live in tandem with his instructions and enjoy his blessings in every aspect of their lives.

In the same way we as children of God by grace through faith, we ought to live by faith. **Ephesians 2:8-10** says, "*For by grace are ye saved through faith; and that not of yourselves: it is the gift of God: 2:9 Not of works, lest any man should boast. 2:10 For we are his workmanship, created in Christ Jesus unto good works, which God hath before ordained that we should walk in them.*"

Romans 1:17 says, "*For therein is the righteousness of God revealed from faith to faith: as it is written, the just shall live by faith*."

When we apply the word of God in every aspect of our lives, the Bible says we shall be blessed in our deeds. **James 1:22-25** says, "*But be ye doers of the word, and not hearers only, deceiving your own selves. 1:23 For if any be a hearer of the word, and not a doer, he is like unto a man beholding his natural face in a glass:*

1:24 For he beholdeth himself, and goeth his way, and straightway forge eth what manner of man he was. 1:25 But whoso looketh into the perfect law of liberty, and continueth therein, he being not a forgetful hearer, but a doer of the work, this man shall be blessed in his deed."

All-round blessing is for only those who apply the word to every aspect of their lives. Make every effort to know the word, and endeavor to consider the word of God and his instructions before you do anything in life. Glory to God!

PRAYER

Dear heavenly Father, I thank you today for the opportunity to study your word. As I live by faith in you through your word I practically experience and enjoy your blessings in every aspect of my life in Jesus' name.

THE BLESSING

Receive power to do the word of God today in Jesus' name. May the devil not take over any aspect of your life in Jesus' name.

THE INVITATION

If you haven't received Jesus as your Lord and Savior, say this prayer now: ***Dear Jesus I believe you are the Son of God and that you died for my sins. Come into my heart and make me a child of God. Thank you for saving me in Jesus' name. Amen.***

Please read Romans 10:9-10

Day 58

Preach The Gospel Of Jesus Everywhere

"And he said unto them, Go ye into all the world, and preach the gospel to every creature. He that believeth and is baptized shall be saved; but he that believeth not shall be damned." (Mark 16:15-16)

As a believer in Christ, we need to live by the totality of the Word of God. In our scriptural text above, Jesus commanded us to go into all the world and preach the gospel, the good news of his death and resurrection for the salvation of sinners. This is our major task in life, we must do it wherever we find ourselves, and it should be our priority.

Our lifestyle, home, dress sense, spending of money and time, etc. should reflect and promote the preaching of the gospel of Jesus always.

Many children of God think more about acquiring the earthly things and forgot our major assignment on earth as a believer, which is the preaching of the gospel of our Lord Jesus Christ. Jesus is THE ONLY WAY OF SALVATION; religion is different from salvation or eternal life. Eternal life is found in Jesus Christ alone.

John 3:16-18 says, *"For God so loved the world, that he gave his only begotten Son, that whosoever believeth in him should not perish, but have everlasting life. 3:17 For God sent not his Son into the world to condemn the world; but that the world through him might be saved. 3:18 He that believeth on him is not condemned: but he that believeth not is condemned already, because he hath not believed in the name of the only begotten Son of God."*

The Bible is very clear on the issue of salvation. Believing in and receiving Jesus as Savior and Lord only can bring salvation and guarantee eternal life. **Acts 4:12** says, *"Neither is there* *salvation in any other: for there is none other name under heaven given among men, whereby we must be saved.*"

It is time to preach the gospel so that the world can hear and receive Jesus as Savior and Lord before his soon coming.

Romans 10:14;17 says, "*How then shall they call on him in whom they have not believed? And how shall they believe in him of whom they have not heard? And how shall they hear without a preacher?... 10:17 so then faith cometh by hearing, and hearing by the word of God.*"

Prayerful presentation of the simple ABC of the gospel is all we need to present to the sinners, and if they believe, they'll be saved. (**Romans 10:9-10**)

GET INVOLVED NOW AND PREACH THE GOSPEL EVERYWHERE IN EVERY POSSIBLE WAY! Hallelujah!

PRAYER

Dear Father thank you for your word and the opportunity to partake of eternal life in Christ. Today as I go about my assignment I made up my mind to let people see Jesus in me and through me. I'm empowered to do this by the Holy Spirit in Jesus' name.

THE BLESSING

May all that is pursuing you for destruction stumble and fall in Jesus' name.

THE INVITATION

If you are not yet saved, sincerely pray this prayer now*: Dear Lord Jesus, I believe you are the Son of God and that you died for my sins, I now receive you as my Savior and confess you as the Lord of my life. I am born again and now a child of God. Hallelujah!*

Please read Romans 10:9-10

Day 59

Give Yourself Wholly To The Things Of God

"Neglect not the gift that is in thee, which was given thee by prophecy, with the laying on of the hands of the presbytery.

Meditate upon these things; give thyself wholly to them; that thy profiting may appear to all." (1Timothy 4:14-15)

As a Christian you are special, you have the gift of God in you according to our opening scripture for today. You have the Holy Spirit living in you. You have another kind of life to live, a life of God prepared for you before the foundation of the world in Christ.

The following scriptures testify to this truth.

1 Peter 2:9 says, "*But ye are a chosen generation, a royal priesthood, an holy nation, a peculiar people; that ye should shew forth the praises of him who hath called you out of darkness into his marvelous light.*"

Ephesians 2:10 also says, "*For we are his workmanship, created in Christ Jesus unto good works, which God hath before ordained that we should walk in them.*"

What you need to do now is to follow the instructions given by the Holy Spirit through Apostle Paul to Bishop Timothy. Meditate on and give yourself wholly, totally, completely to doing them. You must know the word, the things of God, what he expects you to do, and begin to do them continually. Give total attention to the word of God to know, to remember, and to respond accordingly as a child of God. The result is that; your profiting will appear to all to see. Hallelujah!

PRAYER

Dear Father, I thank you today for your word. I receive your word into my spirit and as I meditate continually on it, my life is transforming from glory to glory in Jesus' name. Amen.

THE BLESSING

I pray for you today, may each day of this year bring you favor and glory in Jesus' name.

THE INVITATION

If you haven't received Jesus Christ as your Lord and Savior, pray this prayer now: ***Dear Lord Jesus, I believe you are the Son of God and that you died for my sins. Come into my heart and make me a child of God in Jesus' name. I now received you as my Lord and Savior. I am born again. Glory!***

Please read Romans 10:9-10

Day 60

All Things Are Possible With God

"But Jesus beheld them, and said unto them, With men this is impossible; but with God all things are possible." (Matthew 19:26)

As children of God and joint-heir with Jesus, we are a very special breed of people in this world (**1 Peter 2:9**). In the opening scripture above Jesus tells us that "***With God all things are possible***." Jesus is the truth, he cannot lie. If he said it, then it is so. There is nothing God cannot do. As his children, therefore, we must trust God and live according to his word and become unshakable under any situation or circumstances.

Matthew 7:24-25 says, "***Therefore whosoever heareth these sayings of mine, and doeth them, I will liken him unto a wise man, which built his house upon a rock: 7:25 And the rain descended, and the floods came, and the winds blew, and beat upon that house; and it fell not: for it was founded upon a rock***."

Let us endeavor to do his word, and never do anything contrary to it. To do the word we must know and have it in our heart. We must always read and study the word of God. We must live according to his word; our decisions must be based on the word, so that we can have his backing in all we do.

What is that need in your life today? Begin to trust God now and begin to act based on his words and you shall see the wonders of God in your life.

Luke 1:45 says, "***And blessed is she that believed: for there shall be a performance of those things which were told her from the Lord***." Remember there is nothing impossible with God, just believe God, ask in Faith, and expect a miracle you desire from Him, he will bring it to pass. Believe God for it and start acting and working towards it now. IT IS POSSIBLE WITH GOD!

PRAYER

Father God, we thank you for who you are. You are powerful, merciful, and gracious. Today I received your word into my heart. As I meditate and act upon your word today I live a life of signs and wonders in Jesus' name.

THE BLESSING

May you rise above your troubles in Jesus' name. You shall not be defeated in Jesus' name.

THE INVITATION

If you haven't received Jesus as your Lord and Savior, pray this prayer now: ***Lord Jesus, I believe you are the Son of God and that you died for my sins. Come into my heart and make me a child of God. In Jesus' name I now receive you as my Savior and confess you as the Lord of my life. I am born again. Glory to God!***

Please read Romans 10:9-10

For one on one counseling and prayers visit:

Faith Celebration Christian Centre

(Capchurch Inc.)

1 Ekpiwhre Drive, Opposite Mosheshe Estate, Enerhen (Warri) Delta State, Nigeria.

 Email or call me:

revolubabalola4real@yahoo.ca

Dailytonic16@gmail.com

+2348023883321

+2348075556319

www.ingramcontent.com/pod-product-compliance
Lightning Source LLC
Chambersburg PA
CBHW080817170726
48000CB00021B/3192